EVERYDATA

EVERYDATA

THE MISINFORMATION HIDDEN IN THE *LITTLE DATA* YOU CONSUME EVERY DAY

WHY YOUR GAS TANK ISN'T EMPTY,
YOU'RE NOT BETTER THAN AVERAGE, AND
AFRICA IS BIGGER THAN YOU THINK

WITHDRAWN
JOHN H. JOHNSON, PhD,
AND MIKE GLUCK

bibliomotion
inc.

First published by Bibliomotion, Inc.
39 Harvard Street
Brookline, MA 02445
Tel: 617-934-2427
www.bibliomotion.com

Printed in the United States of America

Library of Congress Cataloging-in-Publication Data

Names: Johnson, John H., author. | Gluck, Mike, author.
Title: Everydata : the misinformation hidden in the little data you consume
    every day / John H. Johnson, Mike Gluck.
Description: First Edition. | Brookline, MA : Bibliomotion, 2016.
Identifiers: LCCN 2015041504 (print) | LCCN 2016004445 (ebook) | ISBN
    9781629561011 (hardback) | ISBN 9781629561028 (ebook) | ISBN 9781629561035
    (enhanced ebook)
Subjects: LCSH: Econometrics. | Consumer behavior. | BISAC: BUSINESS &
    ECONOMICS / Econometrics. | BUSINESS & ECONOMICS / Consumer Behavior. |
    SOCIAL SCIENCE / Popular Culture. | BUSINESS & ECONOMICS / Decision-Making
    & Problem Solving.
Classification: LCC HB139 .J636 2016 (print) | LCC HB139 (ebook) | DDC
    646.7001/5195—dc23
LC record available at http://lccn.loc.gov/2015041504

Dedicated to the memory of my mom, Elizabeth Johnson,
who read the newspaper with reckless abandon, always shared the
most fascinating research studies, and inspired my intellectual curiosity.

—John Johnson

CONTENTS

FOREWORD

In the spring of 2010, the National Football League owners wanted, among *many* other things, to extend the regular season by two games. As executive director of the NFL Players Association (NFLPA), I knew this was a bad idea. More games equal more injuries in a game that already has a 100 percent injury rate. More injuries would mean more careers cut short for athletes whose average careers are already just a little more than three years. Our union faced serious concerns about player safety, compensation, and how to protect the men who, every week during the season, put themselves on the line in America's most beloved sport.

Professional football is a multibillion-dollar industry—and growing. But in 2010–11, facing the first potential work stoppage in over a decade, I needed a sure way to prove that the season needed to remain at sixteen games.

I called John Johnson.

John is an expert on economics, statistics, and data, and he makes even the most complicated data concepts seem simple and straightforward. In short, he is probably one of the smartest guys I know. He is able to explain things carefully and thoughtfully and tailor his explanations to the level of any audience and, most importantly, he's never boring!

Like every football fan in America, the NFLPA wanted to save the upcoming NFL season, so we gave John our data. John and his colleagues developed models that showed when and how often players were injured. They identified the precise plays that had the most serious injuries (leading to the "kickoff rule," which had a dramatic impact on player safety). They estimated the potential economic losses from extending the NFL season to eighteen games—using data to predict how much shorter, on average, each player's career would be. And they worked with us to help quantify the actual value of each NFL game to the surrounding communities, helping us all to better understand the true economic impact of the potential season-ending lockout.

In the end, John's ability to explain the data to our players, the media, and *especially* to the NFL owners (who pay exceptionally close attention to words like "losses"), helped us make decisions to reach our prime objective, safeguarding the health and safety of our players, and eventually conclude contentious negotiations with a ten-year deal historic in its benefits and advantages to the players of the NFL.

This book represents John's thinking at its very best. I am confident that it will help you make better decisions in your everyday life. In these pages, you'll learn how to understand, interpret, and think about all of the data you consume each and every day. Through hundreds of examples, John and his coauthor, Mike Gluck, get right to the heart of the issues, taking the complex and making it easy to picture (and sometimes laugh-out-loud funny). Don't be surprised to find yourself nodding along at every "aha" moment, and questioning every "fact" you see at home and at work.

Here's a fact that can't be denied: the amount of data in your everyday life is growing rapidly and coming at you from every possible direction. That's why it's so important to know how data can be used *and* abused. I've experienced the power of data firsthand, but you don't need to be in sudden-death overtime with some of the wealthiest individuals in the world to see how important it is to understand and manage your data. If you watch TV, go shopping, have a job, or eat at restaurants, then this book is for you. *Everydata* fills a critical void at a critical time, and it does so with great insight, attention, and charm.

This is *your* playbook for becoming a better, smarter, and more confident consumer of data.

Enjoy.

DeMaurice F. Smith
Executive Director
NFL Players Association

PREFACE

Land of 10,000 Questions

What the heck is happening in Minnesota?

During a 10-day span in the summer of 2015, authorities announced three food product recalls for *Salmonella* contamination. All three of these cases were traced back to people who got sick in Minnesota.

The companies involved ended up recalling approximately 3.7 million pounds of chicken products, along with an unspecified amount of yellowfin tuna.[1]

But why Minnesota?

Was all of the contaminated food processed in Minnesota? (No.) Was all of it shipped there? (No.) Are people in Minnesota more likely to get sick from *Salmonella*? (Not that we know of.)

The connection, as Yahoo! Health reported, is simple: Minnesota is just better at identifying cases of foodborne illnesses than other states.[2]

Some people might have heard about three food recalls linked to Minnesota, and assumed the food wasn't safe there.

But that's not the case. If anything, because of the ongoing diligence of Minnesota's Departments of Health and Agriculture, it's quite possible you're better off there than in other areas of the country.

Every day, you're surrounded by media reports and other sources that are often filled with hidden information—and misinformation. This book will help you identify it, interpret it, and become an educated consumer of data (a fancy word for information or facts).

Throughout this book, we'll answer questions like:

- How did a false news report wipe out $136 billion in value from the stock market? (chapter 6)
- Could the Fukushima nuclear disaster have been prevented? (chapter 8)
- What do four out of five pediatricians think about baby food? (chapter 7)
- How do you know which presidential candidate is really leading the polls? (chapter 5)

And, of course...

- Do people who eat grilled cheese sandwiches really have better sex? (chapter 4)

Everydata isn't a real word. Not yet, anyway.

We made it up to describe the tons of *data* that you encounter *every* day.

And we wrote this book to help you get better, smarter, and faster at understanding all of that everydata.

Because even if you're not trained as a data expert, you still have to interpret data. If you're a lawyer, you have to determine if a witness is *cherry-picking* testimony. If you're a nurse, you have to understand if a patient's illness is causing his fever—or if it's simply a *correlation*. If you're a CEO, you want to *predict* how much revenue you'll bring in next quarter. If you're a parent, you want to know if your kid is above (or below) *average*.

This is a book about using the data in your life to make better decisions.

Throughout the book, we will highlight commonly misunderstood data concepts, using real-world and hypothetical examples. At the end of each chapter, we'll give you five ways to start using what you've learned right away. You can read this book straight through, or pick the chapter(s) you're interested in.

This book started as a simple Facebook message between old high school friends John (an economist and statistician) and Mike (a writer) in the fall of 2013.

"Hi Mike—have been kicking around a random idea for a book... wondered if you might have some time to talk."

As John shared his idea for making data concepts easy to understand (based on his experience as a professional economist who has consulted with companies around the world on how to interpret their data) a book outline started to unfold.

"[This] may become our obsession the next year," wrote John.

And so it did. (For the next two years, to be exact.)

One Facebook message became 3,288 notes back and forth, as we discovered that our lives are even more inundated with data than we thought. Everywhere we turned we found more and more examples of data that was misrepresented, misinterpreted, and just plain mistaken.

And here we are. The idea that became an obsession is now a reality. We hope you enjoy it.

Before we start, a quick disclaimer: as a professional economist and statistician, John's day job involves rigorous analysis of data, often as an expert witness for a Fortune 100 company, trade group, or government agency involved in multimillion dollar litigation.[3] This book is a basic overview of essential statistical concepts, not a comprehensive textbook. So if you're opposing counsel looking for some "gotcha" moment, you can stop right now. The good news is that, because this book is meant to be educational *and* entertaining, we get to have some fun—like explaining why your gas tank isn't really empty, why celebrity deaths don't really happen in threes, and why it's okay to drink the milk past the expiration date. So, with that disclaimer out of the way, let's talk data.

1

Data, Data, Everywhere

An Introduction to Everydata

From the moment you open your eyes in the morning, you're surrounded by data. In fact, the average American consumes roughly 34 gigabytes of data every day, according to the "How Much Information?" program at the Global Information Industry Center (part of the University of California, San Diego).[1]

Thirty-four gigabytes is a lot. One gigabyte—or GB, as it's commonly abbreviated—is just over 1 *billion* bytes (a byte is typically equal to one letter or number). If you printed out 34 GB worth of data, it would fill dozens of pickup trucks, said a source cited by the BBC.[2] And that's just from active sources of data at home like your TV, radio, computer, and phone—the 34 GB figure doesn't seem to include data that simply exists around us, or the information we get at work, which could easily double or triple this number.[3]

Let's take a minute and think about all the "everydata" you might encounter—and interpret—just in the first hour or two of your day:

- You open your eyes and see your first data of the day—the glowing numbers on your alarm clock.
  Estimated data consumed: 9 bytes
- You grab your smartphone. It's easy to scan a dozen e-mails, a few texts, some traffic alerts, and breaking news alerts before you even get out of bed.
  Estimated data consumed: 2.1 megabytes (1 megabyte = approximately 1 million bytes)

- You walk into the bathroom, step on the scale, and see the proof that you shouldn't have had pizza last night.
  Estimated data consumed: 3 bytes
- Can you get data from a toothbrush? Sure, if it's one of those electronic ones that vibrates every 30 seconds to remind you to move it around. That vibration is just another type of data.
  Estimated data consumed: 60 bytes
- Ding! A calendar alert on your phone reminds you about a client meeting.
  Estimated data consumed: 43 bytes
- Do you take a multivitamin? Fish oil? Make sure you read the label carefully so you understand all the data it contains. Medicine labels are full of very important data.
  Estimated data consumed: 2.0 megabytes
- Your daughter needs you to sign her math test. How do you know you're seeing all the data? Are there other tests that your daughter doesn't show you? And what do the scores mean—do they correspond with her ability, or are they just capturing her participation or some other measure?
  Estimated data consumed: 46 kilobytes (1 kilobyte = approximately 1,000 bytes)
- How do you get your news in the morning? People actually recall more information when they read a printed newspaper versus reading it online, according to a study from the University of Oregon.[4] As you scan the headlines, you see
  - ➤ The latest poll numbers show 76 percent of Americans disapprove of Congress.
  - ➤ The Red Sox are in first place—winning their 15th game in a row and taking a 7-game lead.
  - ➤ The weather forecast shows a high of 70 degrees Fahrenheit and a low of 58.
  - ➤ A new study shows that drinking a glass of red wine every day will lower your chance of heart disease.
  - ➤ Budget numbers predict that the interest rates will be lowered again by the Federal Reserve.
  Estimated data consumed: 3.1 megabytes

- You wonder what it will cost (in money and time) to refinance your house if interest rates drop. You put a note on an app on your smartphone (which automatically syncs with your computer) and e-mail your spouse.
  Estimated data consumed: 2.2 megabytes
- Time to go to work. As you jump in your car, you're immediately greeted by a dashboard full of data. Is the oil light on or off? How hot or cold is your engine running? What about the tire pressure? Some data is shown via warning lights that are either on or off, some is conveyed with an analog dial, and other data is on a digital screen.
  Estimated data consumed: 63 bytes
- Your gas tank is a quarter full. What exactly does that mean? And why can you still keep driving even when the gauge says empty? (See chapter 6 for the answer.)
  Estimated data consumed: 26 bytes
- At one gas station, the price on the sign is four cents per gallon cheaper than across the street—but the gas station with the cheaper gas only takes cash. Is that four cents per gallon enough to influence your behavior?
  Estimated data consumed: 2.0 megabytes
- Do you take public transportation to work or do you drive? If you're in Washington, D.C., you might use the express lanes on I-495, which charge a "dynamic" toll.[5] (In other words, data is collected and then prices are adjusted accordingly.) But are the toll adjustments following strict rules of supply and demand? Or is this just another example of an institution using hidden data to justify higher prices?
  Estimated data consumed: 44.0 megabytes
- You stop at Starbucks for some coffee. Should you get the 16-ounce Grande or the 20-ounce Venti? You think about the extra cost (and the extra calories). You place your order, then read the label on each little package of Splenda, Sweet'N Low, and Equal; they're all covered with lists of nutrition facts and ingredients. (The real sugar and honey packs don't have nutritional facts on them, making it harder to compare them with their counterparts.)
  Estimated data consumed: 10.1 kilobytes

You're finally at the office, and it's time to get to work. From keeping up with the news to checking your e-mail, reviewing spreadsheets, negotiating contracts, looking at sales forecasts, making phone calls, and going to meetings, it's all data, all day long.

But even this list barely scratches the surface of explaining how data can affect our lives. Because mixed in with data about where to get gas and what to do about your kid's math grade, there's everydata that can influence how happy you'll be, how much money you'll make, and even how long you'll live. For example:

- Where should you buy a house or rent an apartment? Should you pay more attention to school rankings, commute times, crime statistics, potential resale value, or some other data?
- What happens if you have a great job offer on the table and you're trying to decide what to do? What data can you use to justify the salary and benefits you want? When you present your data to your potential new boss, how will she perceive that data?
- How do you decide who to date, and possibly marry? Do you use an online dating service, which filters and interprets your data in order to find a compatible match? Which data is most important to you? Your partner's height? Where he went to college? How much money she makes?
- What if your doctor tells you your blood sugar or cholesterol levels are too high? Is there a specific threshold at which the numbers are dangerous? Are the elevated numbers due to genetics, diet, or some combination of factors? Your doctor may want you to do daily blood tests and keep records of what you eat (more data for you and your doctor to analyze).

So what do you do with it all?

"We're rich in data," noted *Time* magazine, "but the returns are diminishing rapidly, because after a certain point the more information you have, the harder it becomes to extract meaning from it."[6]

Sound familiar? You're not alone.

"LITTLE DATA"

You've probably heard of "big data." It's basically data that's too big for people to process without the use of sophisticated software and computing capacity, given its enormous volume.[7] For example, United Parcel Service, Inc. (UPS) gathers 200 data points per vehicle (it has approximately 100,000 vehicles), using that data to save idling time and fuel, according to a *Bloomberg Business* article, which notes that "a reduction of 1 mile per day for every driver can save the company as much as $50 million a year in fuel, vehicle maintenance and time."[8]

Around the world, big data is being used to solve big problems. The Netherlands is using big data for water management.[9] Food delivery companies use it to satisfy their customers' late-night munchies.[10] IBM is using petabytes of data to identify possible cases of food contamination (1 petabyte = 1 million gigabytes).[11]

Big data is sexy. It makes the headlines. Demand for some big-data-related jobs is increasing more than 80 percent each year, according to an article in *Forbes*.[12] Business school students "can't get enough of big data," says the *Wall Street Journal*, citing the fast-growing number of data-related programs.[13]

But, as you've seen already, it's the little data—the small bits and bytes of data that you're bombarded with in your everyday life—that often has a huge effect on your health, your wallet, your job, your relationships, and so much more, every single day. From food labels to weather forecasts, your bank account to your doctor's office, everydata is all around you.

Unfortunately, people don't always believe the data, even when it's right in front of them.

"Facts don't necessarily have the power to change our minds," said an article in the *Boston Globe*. "In fact, quite the opposite."[14] The article cited a University of Michigan study that found people who were misinformed often held fast to their beliefs; some even felt more strongly in their (false) beliefs when faced with facts. (Apparently, some people simply don't like to admit when they're wrong.)

Still, as the saying goes, the plural of anecdote is not data. Just because all your neighbors say it's the hottest summer ever doesn't mean it's true, for example.

"I think the biggest issue we all face is over-interpreting anecdotal evidence," said Emily Oster, an associate professor of economics at Brown University and the author of *Expecting Better: Why the Conventional Pregnancy Wisdom Is Wrong—and What You Really Need to Know*, when we asked her how people interpret data in their everyday lives.

"People are very drawn to wanting to learn from individual stories or experiences," she added. "It is difficult to force yourself to ignore these anecdotes—or, at a minimum, treat them as just one data point—and draw conclusions from data instead."

Anecdotes may be memorable. They may be persuasive. But it's important to pay attention to the facts.

A LITTLE CONTEXT

Here's something else to keep in mind—in everyday life, you may be looking at data in context, or comparing it to the other data around you. Sometimes this context and additional data helps, other times it may be misleading.

Consider:

■ In the city of Hermosa Beach, California, the average estimated response time for the fire department was just over five minutes.[15] Is that a good response time or not? In order to interpret the data, you may want to compare it to the city's response times in the past, response times from similar communities, and other data.

■ Authorities at George Bush International Airport in Houston were getting complaints about passengers' luggage taking too long to arrive. So they moved the baggage claim area farther away from the gates. Passengers then spent the time walking—not waiting—and complaints dropped, as people perceived the time to get their bags as being shorter.

■ There are differences in the way we consume and interpret data in different mediums. For example, do you feel that the *Washington Post* website is more accurate than the printed version of the newspaper, because it can be updated nearly instantly? Do you prefer reading a printed magazine because you can rip out interesting articles? Does a hardcover book feel more authoritative than a paperback, even though they're both printed?

As Seth Godin asked in a blog post, "What tastes better, a $30 bottle of wine that's the cheapest the restaurant offers...or the very same bottle at the restaurant next door, where it's the most expensive?"[16] Context matters.

Then, of course, there's all the hidden data, which you may not even know about. For example, if you were checking the Weather Channel app on a humid day a few summers ago, you might have seen an ad for Pantene Pro-V Smooth shampoo (designed to tame frizzy hair) as the *Wall Street Journal* reported.[17] Perhaps the ad seemed like a coincidence, but in reality it was specifically targeted to women based on the weather in their zip code. If the humidity (which makes hair get frizzy) was high, the ad appeared. If the humidity was low, an ad for a different hair care product appeared. You could see the weather, and you could see the ad, but unless you worked for the Weather Channel you probably wouldn't see the connection between the two. In a data-driven world, you don't always know what's driving the data.

AN EDUCATED CONSUMER OF DATA

If you're from New York or New Jersey, you may remember the commercials for SYMS clothing stores, in which Sy Syms told viewers that "An educated consumer is our best customer." (Fun fact: Sy changed his last name to "Syms" after the store.)[18]

Sy was right. An educated consumer (of data, in this case) is far ahead of the rest.

Your job as an informed data consumer is to keep asking questions and understand how the data you're seeing can affect your life. You need to ask yourself:

- What is the political candidate not telling you in his TV commercial?
- Is a reporter using accurate sample data—or is she only sharing the data that supports her story?
- Which data is the sales forecast based on?
- Did your doctor say that your disease was caused by certain behavior—or only that there's a link?
- What is the marketer emphasizing on the product package and why is that data highlighted?
- Why does the annual report show some data in pie charts, but the rest in bar graphs?

Sometimes the data is trying to sell you something—whether it's a product, a service, or a point of view. In these cases, simply knowing that the newscaster wants your attention, the advertiser wants your money, and the politician wants your vote may help you be a better consumer of data. But sometimes there is no agenda—just data that you need to make sense of in order to understand the world around you.

And that—in a nutshell—is what this book is about: helping you recognize all the "everydata" in your life, showing you how to interpret it, and offering proven tips for avoiding common data traps so you can become an educated consumer of data—and make better decisions in your everyday life.

Here we go.

2

The *Challenger* Challenge
How Sampling Can Affect Results

In one cruel moment, our exhilaration turned to horror; we waited and watched and tried to make sense of what we had seen."[1]

On January 31, 1986, President Ronald Reagan stood outside the Johnson Space Center, addressing the family, friends, and colleagues of the seven astronauts who had died earlier that week, when the space shuttle *Challenger* broke apart in midair.

Over the next few months, experts spent countless hours interviewing key witnesses, examining the evidence, and documenting their findings.

And ultimately, it came down to data.

The managers in charge of the shuttle launch made a classic error. They focused on the wrong data. And seven national heroes "slipped the surly bonds of earth."[2]

JANUARY 28, 1986

Here's what happened, according to a book that covered the incident: "On the morning of 28 January 1986, the Space Shuttle Challenger, mission 51–L, rose into the cold blue sky over the Cape. To exuberant spectators and breathless flight controllers, the launch appeared normal. Within 73 seconds after liftoff, however, the external tank ruptured, its liquid fuel exploded, and Challenger broke apart."[3]

"The specific failure," noted the *Report of the Presidential Commission on the Space Shuttle Challenger Accident,* "was the destruction of the seals that are intended to prevent hot gases from leaking...."[4] Investigators quickly focused their attention on a key part of the seals—the rubber O-rings that went in between two sections of the solid rocket motor—the "tang" and the "clevis."

The O-rings on the *Challenger* needed to be flexible enough to compress and expand, sometimes within milliseconds. But O-ring resiliency "is directly related to its temperature...a warm O-ring will follow the opening of the tang-to-clevis gap. A cold O-ring may not."[5] In fact, investigators found that a compressed O-ring is five times more responsive at 75 degrees Fahrenheit than at 30 degrees Fahrenheit.

The air temperature at launch was 36 degrees Fahrenheit.[6]

The commission's report (often called the Rogers Commission Report after chairman and former secretary of state William P. Rogers) found "it is probable" that the O-rings were not compressing and expanding as needed. The resulting gap allowed the gases to escape, destroying the *Challenger,*[7] and showing that "even our nation's largest achievements could be undone by something as mundane as an O-ring...."[8]

So why didn't engineers stop the launch, given the cold temperatures?

They tried. Bob Lund was a vice president of engineering for Morton Thiokol, the contractor that supplied the solid rocket motor. The night before the fateful launch, he and others recommended against launching the *Challenger* in cold weather (a recommendation that was later reversed).[9]

"We were concerned the temperature was going to be lower than the 50 or the 53 that had flown the previous January, and we had experienced some...erosion on the O-rings...it wasn't a major concern, but we said, gee, you know, we just don't know how much further we can go below the 51 or 53 degrees or whatever it was. So we were concerned with the unknown."[10]

In other words—they didn't have enough data. Nobody knew what would happen to the O-rings on a day where the temperature was 15 degrees colder than that of any previous launch.[11]

But not having data below 53 degrees was just one of the issues.

UNDERSTANDING SAMPLE SELECTION

When you conduct a statistical analysis on a sample of the available data, you can induce what in statistics is known as a *sample selection* problem. Running an analysis on less than the entire data set is not always a problem, but it can lead to mistaken conclusions depending on the question you are trying to answer. In this case, the data was limited only to failures. But the possibility of a failure was exactly the question of interest.

The team recognized that they didn't have data below 53 degrees, and decided to look at all cases where there had been signs of O-ring distress, regardless of temperature. The conclusion the scientists and engineers drew based on this data was correct. But the problem, as you'll see, was that they did not study the *right* data for the question they needed to answer. In this case, they should have looked at *all* of the data on O-ring performance—not just cases where there were signs of distress.

The night before the disaster—as engineers tried to convince their managers at Thiokol and NASA not to launch—someone pointed out that there had been signs of O-ring distress on a shuttle that was launched at 75 degrees.

It's true—there had been issues at 75 degrees. And at 70 degrees. And at 63 degrees. In fact, on seven separate missions, there was evidence of O-ring thermal distress. And if you look at the temperature for these launches, you'll see that there is no easily recognizable pattern. Observing this data, you could easily be convinced that temperature does *not* affect O-ring performance.[12] As the Rogers Commission Report stated, "In such a comparison, there is nothing irregular in the distribution of O-ring 'distress' over the spectrum of joint temperatures at launch between 53 degrees Fahrenheit and 75 degrees Fahrenheit."

The problem is that this comparison *only* looks at data from 7 out of the 24 space shuttle launches up to that point. By focusing only on the flights *with* O-ring incidents, people were truncating the data set—a fancy way of saying that they weren't looking at all of the data. And that error in how the data was analyzed would have significant repercussions.

Because the engineers only looked at "failed launches—they missed a vital connection that becomes obvious when you look at the

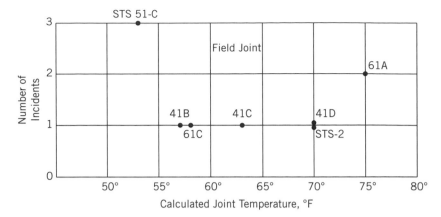

FIGURE 2-1   This chart shows the flights that had incidents of O-ring thermal distress (defined as O-ring erosion, blow-by, or excessive heating). Note that it only shows flights that had this O-ring distress, and that they are plotted by temperature.

temperatures for the seven prior launches with problems *and* the 17 prior launches without problems," explained Ann E. Tenbrunsel and Max H. Bazerman in a blog post for *Freakonomics*.[13]

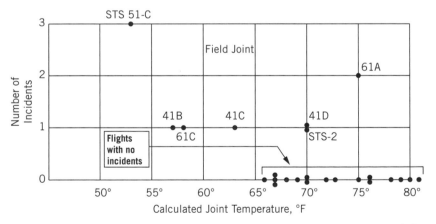

FIGURE 2-2   This chart shows all flights—those with O-ring distress, and those without. Again, flights are plotted by temperature.

When you look at all of the data—including flights with zero incidents—you can see the difference for yourself.

Above 65 degrees, only 3 out of 20 flights had incidents.

Below 65 degrees, *all 4 flights* had incidents.

This is a classic example of how reliance on a sample of data—even with the best intentions—can contribute to disastrous results.[14]

Fortunately, you probably won't ever be in a position where the sample of data you choose could lead to the loss of seven lives and the destruction of a spacecraft that cost $1.7 billion to rebuild.[15] But you will face these types of data problems every day, whether you're reading the newspaper at home or putting together a report at work. In the following pages, we'll explain what sampling is, and show you how to avoid drawing incorrect inferences.

WHY DO WE NEED TO SAMPLE?

Let's say you have a box of 100 crayons, and you want to know how many of them are blue. In this case, you need to make 100 *observations* to gather all of the data. An *observation* is simply the act of looking at one unit.

With a box of 100 crayons, it's feasible to study the full *population* by making an observation about each and every crayon. Looking at the full population can be beneficial, because then you don't have to make assumptions about what's happening with the rest of the data.

But what if you've been really, really good all year, and on your birthday you get a box filled with one million crayons? Now, your full population is one million.

Who has time to look at one million crayons?

Fortunately, there is an alternative: with a little statistical analysis, you can get an estimate of how many blue crayons there are. How? You can take a *sample* of the full population. A sample is some (but not all) of the full population. Once you have your sample, you can make inferences about the full population. (But, as you've seen from the space shuttle *Challenger* example, how you select your sample has huge implications for your data analysis.)

Using a sample to estimate results in the full population is common in data analysis. But you have to be careful, because even small mistakes can quickly become big ones, given that each observation represents many others. There are also many factors you need to consider if you want to make sure your inferences are accurate. And, as we'll discuss in chapter 5, ultimately you'll want to know if the sample you've drawn tells you anything statistically about the population.

WHAT IF?

The process of making statistical conclusions about the data is called drawing an *inference*. In any statistical analysis, if you're going to draw an inference, the goal is to make sure you have the right data to answer the question you are asking. In this chapter, we're going to explore two of the more important types of sampling issues we want you to be aware of as an informed consumer of data.[16]

First, you need to think about whether the universe of data that is being studied or collected is *representative of the underlying population*. This type of problem has to do with how the data is collected and what data is collected. Back to our crayon example: what if whoever packed the crayon box put more blue ones on one side—which is where you pulled your sample from? In this case, when you try to estimate how many blue crayons are in the box, you will think there are a lot more than you realized, because the underlying data is not representative of the entire box of crayons. You are studying a sample that is biased toward blue crayons.

Second, you need to consider what you are analyzing in the data that has been collected—*are you analyzing all of the data, or only part of it?* For example, let's say you had data on every crayon in the box, and you want to determine how many of the crayons are blue. But in your analysis, you only count a crayon as blue if it has "blue" in the name. In this case, your choice to only study part of the data (the name of the crayon) would likely lead to a very different estimate of the universe of blue crayons, compared with someone who looked at the color of each crayon and included colors such as aqua, turquoise, and denim in the results.

You always have to ask—can you accurately extend your findings from the sample to the general population? That's called *external validity*—when you can extend the results from your sample to draw meaningful conclusions about the full population.

The examples in this chapter highlight many of the ways in which data is sampled—sometimes correctly, sometimes not. For the purposes of this chapter, we're going to assume that any errors related to sampling were, for the most part, inadvertent or unintentional. That's an important distinction, because sometimes data is purposely sampled in a way to derive a given result, or *cherry-picked*—a concept we discuss in much more detail in chapter 7.

As you can see, when it comes to understanding everydata, sampling is the foundation that everything else is built on. If there's a problem with the sample, you're going to have issues down the road when you try to interpret your data. There are data experts who spend their entire professional careers crafting sample sets that are accurate, representative, and can provide the basis for sound statistical analysis. These folks are worth their weight in gold, because without them, everything else crumbles.

WEIRD SCIENCE

If you're studying human behavior, you have to use sampling. There's simply no way to observe the more than seven billion people on our planet.

So how do you choose a sample?

Ideally, you would want a large, diverse group of people whose members accurately represent the full population. Unfortunately, that's not what happens in psychology. Not even close.

As one journal article noted, "Behavioral scientists routinely publish broad claims about human psychology and behavior in the world's top journals based on samples drawn entirely from Western, Educated, Industrialized, Rich, and Democratic (WEIRD) societies."[17]

But wait—it gets worse. Many studies are based not just on WEIRD people but on some of the WEIRDest of them all—Americans.

As one researcher noted, "a striking feature of research in American psychology is that its conclusions are based not on a broad cross-section of humanity but on a small corner of the human population—mainly, persons living in the United States."[18]

The United States is less than 5 percent of the world's population—but was home to 68 percent of the samples, in one researcher's study. "The rest of the world's population, the other 95%, is neglected."[19]

While Americans are accustomed to being in the spotlight, surely you can understand why it's troubling to conduct research about people using a sample that neglects most of them. Especially because Americans are unlikely to be representative of the rest of the world, at least along many dimensions. Living in the U.S. (and other WEIRD countries) may affect everything from the way we perceive images to our relationship with money.[20] In fact, as one researcher put it, WEIRD people may be "one of the worst subpopulations one could study for generalizing about *Homo sapiens*."[21]

But wait—there's more.

Here in the U.S., a study has found that most psychology research "is consistently done primarily on college students—specifically, undergraduate students taking a psychology course. It's been this way for the better part of 50 years."[22]

In one journal, two-thirds of the American studies that were published used undergrad psychology students as samples.[23]

On some level, using this sample set makes sense. Undergrad psych students are already roaming the halls of every college. They're willing to work for beer money. And, in many cases, that makes them "good enough" for researchers.[24]

Except that they're not. Undergrad psych students are younger than the average American, to give just one example of how they may be different. When a random American undergrad is "more than 4,000 times more likely to be a research participant than is a randomly selected person from outside of the West,"[25] that's not just WEIRD. It may lead you to the wrong conclusion about many of the psychological phenomena you want to study.

BIGGER ISN'T ALWAYS BETTER

Having a large sample size doesn't guarantee better results if it's the wrong large sample. You could study the behavior of every psychology undergrad in the world, but that doesn't mean you can make accurate inferences about the full population of human beings.

Consider the National Weight Control Registry (NWCR), which bills itself as the largest prospective investigation of long-term successful weight loss maintenance, tracking more than 10,000 people. But being "the largest" doesn't mean it's a good sample set, any more than going to the largest buffet in Las Vegas makes you a healthy eater. Yes, your chances of eating something healthy go up the more items you put on your plate—but you have to dig deeper to understand the data. And when you dig into the NWCR's published research findings about weight loss, you'll see that many of them are based on studies in which women outnumber men by a sizable margin.[26] That's not surprising, given that 80 percent of the people in the registry are women, and only 20 percent are men.[27]

Does this invalidate their findings? Not necessarily.

Does it mean their sample set isn't valid? Not necessarily.

But it does limit the conclusions that can be extrapolated about weight loss to the broader population. Even with a large number of people, these individuals are still a specific group—participants who have lost weight, volunteered to be in the study groups, and have certain characteristics. It's just an example of why you can't assume anything about your data—no matter how large your sample size is.

STRAP YOURSELF IN

The headline in the *Los Angeles Times* would make any parent with young children stop and take a second look.

"High chair injuries up 22% in 7 years; how to keep your baby safe."[28]

At first glance, it all seems legit, right? After all, the *LA Times* is one of the largest, most respected newspapers in the country. The article was based on a study published in the peer-reviewed journal *Clinical Pediatrics*. Its lead author directed the Center for Injury Research and Policy at the Research Institute at Nationwide Children's Hospital, one of the top 10 hospitals of its kind for National Institutes of Health funding.[29]

The data for the study came from the National Electronic Injury Surveillance System (NEISS), which collects patient information from hospitals. The sample set didn't include data from pediatricians. It didn't include data from parents. It only included data from hospitals—and even then, only from some of them.[30] In other words, the results only represent *some* of the injuries linked to high chairs.

Earlier in this chapter—with the space shuttle *Challenger*—we saw how experts only looked at *some* of the data they had. Here, it seems that the experts looked at *all* of the data they had in the NEISS data set. But the problem was that *even with all the data they had* (injuries that led to hospital visits), *they didn't have all the data* (all injuries). And without all of the data, in this case, it was difficult to answer the key questions people might care about.

To be fair, NEISS seems like a logical source of data if you're studying high chair injuries. And both the authors of the study and the *LA Times* reporter were clear about where the data came from. But that doesn't change the way we need to approach the information, as smart consumers of data.

For example, what if it were the case that during the course of the study, fewer kids were hurt in high chair accidents overall, but the total number of kids taken to the hospital after a high chair accident went up? In this scenario, fewer kids were hurt overall, but a higher percentage of parents whose kids were hurt decided to go to the hospital. Why? Maybe more parents were aware of concussion risks because of a high-profile news story. Maybe there was a new research study, and more pediatricians were encouraging parents to go to the hospital. Maybe there were actually fewer injuries, but the injuries that did occur were more serious. If you don't ask why, you'll never know how much credit to give the claim and how to interpret it correctly.

Just to be clear, it's not that we don't want kids to be safe. We're both (over)protective parents—the kind who study crash test rankings before buying a minivan.[31] We're just saying that you need to know where your data comes from.

And if you're responsible for a kid, make sure you use the safety restraints on the high chair; most of the injuries happened when kids tried to stand up in a high chair or climb out of it.[32]

WE'RE NUMBER 1! AND NUMBER 58!

Syracuse University is number 1—in the Princeton Review ranking of party schools.[33]

Syracuse University is also tied for number 58—in the *U.S. News & World Report* ranking of national universities.[34]

Even though each list is looking at the same school, they're sampling completely different data to ask totally different questions. It's brains versus bongs. *U.S. News* looks at graduation rates, strength of the faculty, and other key metrics. The party school rankings are based on student surveys that ask about alcohol and drug use, fraternity/sorority life, and similar factors.

Sure, we could fill this chapter with reasons why we shouldn't compare these lists (different methodologies, etc.). And you should absolutely question how each group arrived at its rankings.

But the point is simple: you can look at the same exact person, place, or thing completely differently based on what data you use for your sample and what questions you are asking.

NO SELFIES

How many times did you eat junk food last week?

How much TV did you watch last month?

How fast were you *really* driving?

When you ask people for information about themselves, you run the risk of getting flawed data. People aren't always honest. We have all sorts of biases. Our memories are far from perfect. With self-reported data, you're assuming that "8" on a scale of 1 to 10 is the same for all people (it's not). And you're counting on people to have an objective understanding of their behavior (they don't). (For a more thorough look at the perils of self-reported data, read "The Dangers of Self-Report" on the British Science Foundation *Brainwaves* blog.)[35]

The result of all this potential uncertainty is that self-reported data may be unreliable. Most of us say we're better drivers than average, according to a study in the *Journal of Safety Research*.[36] We overreport our height and underreport our weight, another report found.[37] These things can happen when you ask people to make observations about themselves.

Sometimes, self-reported data is the only data available. Sometimes, it's just easier to collect. Self-reported data isn't always bad; it depends in part on the context, the collection methods, and the way questions are asked. It's just one more thing to watch out for, if you're going to be a smart consumer of data.

ELECTORAL KNOWLEDGE

The next president of the United States may owe his (or her) victory to sampling.

You see, the president has to win the majority of votes in the Electoral College. These votes are based in part on the U.S. Census.[38] And the U.S. Census relies on sampling to get accurate numbers.

That's because every 10 years, as per the Constitution, the U.S. Census counts every resident in the United States.[39]

Except it doesn't.

It would be virtually impossible to observe the full population by counting every single person from sea to shining sea. As the Census Bureau says on its own website, "In a Census, some people are not counted."[40] As *Time* magazine reported, "The 1990 census missed an estimated 8 million people—mostly immigrants and urban minorities— and it managed to double-count 4 million white Americans."[41]

Why does it matter? Beyond elections, the federal government uses census numbers to allocate funds and support to communities. The more people you have, the more support you should get.

The city of Anaheim lost $1.5 million in federal funding when the city was undercounted by more than 7,000 people in the 1990 census, according to Congresswoman Loretta Sanchez. That money would have made a big difference for Anaheim—or nearly any city. "It would have made our streets safer, we would have had shelter for the homeless, we could have trained the unemployed."[42]

Unlike other examples in this chapter, this isn't a story illustrating sampling done incorrectly or interpreted improperly. Rather, it's meant to illustrate the (often unseen) *impact* of sampling. When the person who sits in the Oval Office could be there because of sampled data—or your streets could have fewer police officers because of sampling—we think it's something you should know about.

SEPARATING THE WHEAT FROM THE CHAFF

Consider the recent gluten-free craze in the United States. Headlines abound about the latest diet craze to avoid gluten, a protein found in wheat that is known to give dough its elasticity.

But how many people in the U.S. are gluten free?

According to a marketing study by the NPD Group, more than 29 percent of Americans are trying to avoid gluten in their diets.[43] Given the recent popularity of the gluten-free movement, the potential market for gluten-free products is estimated to be more than 44 million people.[44] (Astute readers may notice that 29 percent of the population is much more than 44 million people; this disparity is likely due to differing methodologies in collecting the data—not to mention the distinction between people who are trying to avoid gluten versus people who will actually purchase gluten-free products.)

Now, compare that to the number of people who actually suffer from celiac disease—the underlying condition that relates to the inability of the small intestine to absorb gluten. According to the National Foundation for Celiac Awareness, 1 in 133 people suffer from the disease—approximately 2.4 million people in the United States, or less than 1 percent.[45]

This is an example where a study of the entire population would give dramatically different results than the potential effects on the relevant subset of the population who matters—those with celiac disease or gluten sensitivity. As explained by Dr. David Katz in the *Huffington Post,* there is a group of people who can feel better by removing gluten from their diets, and a smaller group of people for which it is "potentially even a matter of life and death" to eliminate gluten. "For everyone else, going gluten free is at best a fashion statement."[46]

The fact that many people suffer from celiac disease is a serious problem. But our point is that you can get two very different answers to the same question ("How many people are gluten free?") based on the population you're sampling—and the criteria you use when asking. If you ask the full population if they're *trying* to be gluten free, you get 29 percent. If you ask the Celiac Awareness group how many people have the disease that *requires* them to be gluten free, you get fewer than 1 percent. Similarly, the results from a study that focused on the lack of health effects of a gluten-free diet for the entire population could be very dangerous if they were then applied to the less than 1 percent of the population who could potentially die from eating gluten.

Big difference.

FILL IN THE BLANKS

Sometimes, the data just isn't all there.

Consider this example from Chicago Public Schools, the third-largest district in the United States. The school system publishes reams of data showing how well its students perform.[47] It also uses data to determine student growth, which is a part of teacher evaluation ratings and principal evaluation ratings, and a factor in school accountability.[48]

But if you study the 2014 NWEA Measures of Academic Progress (MAP) data, you may notice that some charter schools didn't provide results.[49] In fact, if you scroll through the 8,322 lines in the Excel document, you'll see quite a few instances where there is simply no data recorded. Just blank cells.

Why? In some cases, it appears that the charter schools were new, or had extremely small class sizes (or possibly both), so it makes sense that they didn't have any data to supply.

But in other cases, the charter schools had been open for 5 or even 10 years. The data—presumably—was there. It appears as if these schools simply didn't report it. As one Chicago school principal noted in a piece for the *Chicago Sun-Times,* "I was told these charters had not 'opted in' to the MAP assessment... [Chicago Public Schools] allows some charter schools not to participate in the assessment used to hold regular public schools accountable."[50] (Public schools do not appear to have the option of opting out.)

It's quite possible the missing data wouldn't have made a significant difference in the overall comparison.[51] But when you read a headline that says, "CPS outpaces charter schools in improvements, especially in reading,"[52] you can see how data-based stories can change our opinions and affect our behavior.

If the underlying data isn't sampled accurately, it's like building a house on a foundation that's missing a few chunks of concrete. Maybe it won't matter. But if the missing concrete is in the wrong spot—or if there is too much concrete missing—the whole house can come falling down.

WHAT'S MISSING?

Sometimes, you can't sample the right data because it doesn't exist.

When President Obama had to decide whether to launch the raid to capture Osama bin Laden, it was "a very difficult decision, in part because the evidence that we had was not absolutely conclusive. This was circumstantial evidence that he was gonna be there."[53]

In other words, he didn't have all the data.

This happens all the time—in politics and in business, at school and at home. You have a data set, but you know it's incomplete. (Which is still often better than thinking your data set is complete when it's not.)

So the next time you're trying to make a decision, ask yourself: What data do you wish you had? What data could change your mind? We're not saying you should wait to have all the data before you make any decision, because then you'd never go on a first date, or try sushi. But the more you know about what you don't know, the better off you'll be.

Being a Good Consumer of Sampled Data

1. **Understand the consequences of drawing conclusions based on the wrong sample.** Is the sample representative of the population? For example, who are the individuals who were surveyed? Was the data selected based on a key outcome you are trying to study, and how might studying this "sample" influence the analysis?

2. Ask yourself: **What data is the most appropriate** to answer the question that is being asked? For example, at one point the *Challenger* team looked only at flights with O-ring incidents, which was probably not the most appropriate data to answer the question, since it showed these incidents spread out over a temperature range. If they had focused on all flights, they may have seen that the O-ring incidents occurred more frequently within the lower temperatures. If you were trying to answer a question about human behavior, what would be the types of people that you would want to know were included? Or, put differently, how might the people who were asked the questions affect the results of the particular analysis?

3. When reading about a new finding or study in the newspaper, ask yourself: **What data was used to draw the conclusions**? Who was asked the questions, or who was the basis of the study? When you see phrases like "In an unscientific survey…" or "leading _____," consider them to be red flags. You could ask your five-year-old who he thinks should be our next president and publish the results as "an unscientific survey." And "leading" is one of those words that sounds good but is difficult to quantify ("leading what?" you might ask).

4. **Beware of self-reported data**—it's often easier to ask people about what they ate, what they watched, or how they behaved than it is to observe them and record their actions. But self-reported data is not

always the most accurate. Keep this in mind when you're looking at data that was supplied by the subjects of the study.

5.   Finally, remember that, as with many statistical issues, **sampling in and of itself is not a good or a bad thing**. Sampling is a powerful tool that allows us to learn something, when looking at the full population is not feasible (or simply isn't the preferred option). And you shouldn't be misled to think that you always should use all the data. In fact, using a sample of data can be incredibly helpful. There are contexts where focusing on a subset of the data to draw conclusions is meaningful and appropriate. (As Arthur Nielsen Sr.—founder of the ACNielsen company—reportedly said, "If you don't believe in sampling, the next time you have a blood test, ask them to take it all out."[54]) There are other cases where the results that we are studying are driven by the specific data set we are analyzing. Neither is a problem in and of itself—but how the results are interpreted, and what they mean, is the key.

3

Red State Blues

Averages and Aggregates—A Closer Look at Summary Statistics

You may know El Paso, Texas, as the home of the Texas Showdown Festival, the biggest tattoo and music festival in West Texas. Or maybe you think it's where the Steve Miller Band ran into a great big hassle.[1]

If you're a politician, however, you may know El Paso as one of many places where votes are counted, but they don't always count.

Huh?

Consider this—in the 2012 presidential election, Barack Obama received 70 percent of the vote in El Paso County (where El Paso is located). His main opponent, Mitt Romney, got 28 percent of the vote.[2] In fact, Barack Obama received more than three million votes in Texas.

Yet none of them made a difference in the outcome of the election, because of the way the data was counted.

We all know that you don't mess with Texas. So what happened?

Statistics. That's what.

As we mentioned earlier in the book, the United States uses the Electoral College, an institution that results in a winner-take-all system for each state most of the time. In most cases, a presidential candidate receives *all* of a state's Electoral College votes for winning that state's popular vote. As a result, we have "red states"—those in which the Electoral College votes go to the Republican Party candidate—and "blue states," which go for the Democrats.

Yes, Obama received more than three million votes in Texas in 2012. But Romney had more than four million. And so Romney got *all* of Texas's electoral college votes.

The Electoral College is an example of *aggregated data*—a type of *summary statistic* that can often be misleading because it can mask variation in the data. You've probably seen media reports that analyze all of the supposed differences between red states and blue states, with stories highlighting differences in everything from job creation to environmental regulations to Obamacare.[3] But is there really that much of a divide in terms of the way we think, act, and vote? Or will we see a different story as we go deeper into the data?

Let's take a closer look at the voting data, starting with a map of the 2012 election results (figure 3-1) from Mark Newman at the University of Michigan (note that red is light gray and blue is dark gray in this map).[4]

When you look at red states versus blue states, you see lots of divisions. Florida, for example, is the lone blue state in the entire Southeast. But that's because you are seeing the data *aggregated* at the state level. In other words, all you're seeing is the winner-take-all nature of the Electoral College.[5]

Even in states that are decidedly red or blue, there may be large numbers of voters who vote the opposite way. Newman illustrated this point

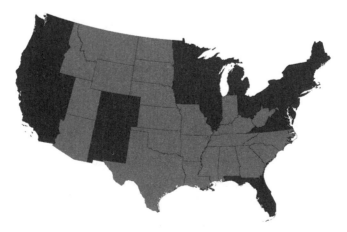

FIGURE 3-1   Red states are light gray; blue states are dark gray.

FIGURE 3-2   Red counties are light gray; blue counties are dark gray.

perfectly with a series of maps that disaggregated the 2012 state results. In this one (figure 3-2), he shows us the results county by county.[6] Look closely, and you'll see El Paso County as a speck of blue (dark gray) on the western tip of Texas.

Now, as we look at vote counts of smaller units (counties) rather than bigger units (states), the map doesn't look quite as divisive. With a few exceptions (hi, Vermont!) most states are a mixture of blue and red.

(We should note that not everyone votes for the Democrat or Republican. For example, in 2012 there were 67,326 Americans—roughly the population of Redondo Beach, California—who voted for Roseanne Barr. Yes, that Roseanne Barr.)[7]

Of course, even these county-by-county results still only show the aggregate vote total (Democrat versus Republican) within each county. So Newman went a step further, and used shades of purple (which we've converted to gray, on our maps here) to show how *strongly* each county went for a candidate, based on the percentages of votes. This is still aggregated data at the county level, but now we have added another layer of disaggregation—how strongly a county went for a candidate. Here, in figure 3-3, Newman further blurs the red–blue divide, and offers an even more nuanced view of the political landscape. El Paso County is a dark shade of gray (deep blue), which reflects the fact that Obama received 70 percent of the vote (actually, 69.84 percent).

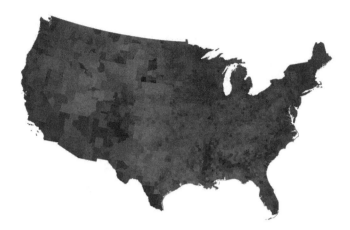

FIGURE 3-3

The three maps in this section all use the same election results data. They all summarize a count of the votes, but they use different levels of aggregation. As a result, they tell a more (or less) nuanced story of voter preferences depending on both how and how much of the data is being aggregated.

The way in which data is aggregated can mask important variations. Aggregating data at the statewide level makes Texas a red state. But aggregating at the county level would make some counties in Texas blue. In this chapter, we will explore some of the common statistical ways that people summarize data, and how aggregate measures can mask important variation in the underlying data sets.

MIND THE (DATA) GAP

The World Happiness Report bills itself as "a landmark survey of the state of global happiness."[8] Published by an offshoot of the United Nations, the report is read by more than a million people each year, and is covered by major media outlets around the globe.

Led by Switzerland at number one, the top of the list reads like a Who's Who from the Winter Olympics podium, with Norway, Canada, and Sweden all taking top spots.

Scroll down, and you'll see the United Kingdom, tucked in as the 21st happiest country in the world. It's a respectable ranking, putting the U.K. ahead of Germany, France, and Spain, but still behind former territories New Zealand and Australia.[9]

As you look through the 172-page report, you can read all about the researchers' methodology and results. You can (and you should) ask questions about how researchers sampled the population and interpreted the results.

But what caught our attention is the notion of comparing one whole country to another. By doing this—looking at an entire nation as one entity—the World Happiness Rankings uses an *average* ranking for each country.

An average is a summary measure that reporters, researchers, and others can use to capture some aspect of the data. It's like a camera that can take a picture and offer some perspective, but only from one direction at a time. Just as with aggregated data, an average is a summary statistic that can tell you *something* about the data—but it is only one metric, and oftentimes a deceiving one at that. By taking all of the data and boiling it down to one value, an average (and other summary statistics) may imply that all of the underlying data is the same, even when it's not.

Because the U.K. gathers its own happiness data through the U.K.'s Office for National Statistics (ONS), we can take a more granular look at the data, rather than examining just the nationwide average we see in the World Happiness Rankings. And, as you might expect, when you take a closer look, happiness varies across the U.K. On a scale of 1 to 10, different regions had different scores, including:[10]

7.0 – North Lanarkshire (Scotland)
7.2 – Northeast region of England
7.6 – Gwynedd (Wales) and Cheshire East UA (England)
7.9 – Eilean Siar, Orkney, and Shetland (Scotland)

(Of course, even these numbers are still simply averages of the local population. It's quite possible that they would vary by specific neighborhood or based on other variables such as gender, income, and age. And, for those of you who are interested, the U.K. had an average score of 7.3, according to the ONS.)

We're not trying to compare the ONS data and *World Happiness Report* data—nor should we, since they appear to use different methodologies, cover different time frames, and have other disparities. Instead, we're using these two sources to show how an average can mask differences throughout the data.

Everyone in the U.K. is not the same. The Beatles are not the Rolling Stones. But a national average binds them all together by geography, regardless of their differences.

KNOW WHAT I MEAN?

Statistically speaking, here are three different terms you should know when thinking about averages: mean, median, and mode.

The *mean* is what most people think of when you say "average." To get the mean, you add up all the values, then divide by the number of data points.

The *median* is the middle value. If you arrange your data points from smallest to largest, the median is the one right in the middle. (If you have an even number of data points, it's the mean of the two points closest to the middle.)

The *mode* is the data point (or points) most commonly found in your data. If no data point appears more than once, then there is no mode. On the other hand, you can have multiple modes if there are two (or more) data points that both repeat the same number of times.

Let's look at some sample data to see how it works.[11]

Imagine it's 2013 and you live in the Chelsea Apartments in Seattle. The building—which was supposedly built as a hotel for the Seattle World's Fair—has 10 apartment units.[12]

Now, let's say 9 of the units are occupied by you and your friends (one person per unit), and (coincidentally) you all earn the same exact amount that year—$50,000.

One day, Bill Gates decides to downsize (a lot) and moves into the

10th unit. He earns $11.5 billion that year.[13] To calculate the average (mean) earnings of all 10 people in the building, you start by adding up everyone's annual earnings: $50,000 + $50,000 + $50,000 + $50,000 + $50,000 + $50,000 + $50,000 + $50,000 + $50,000 + $11,500,000,000 = $11,500,450,000. Then, you simply divide by the number of people (10) to get a mean annual earnings of $1,150,045,000.

Now, to calculate the *median* earnings of all 10 people, you arrange your data from smallest to largest and pick the data point in the middle.

1: $50,000
2: $50,000
3: $50,000
4: $50,000
5: $50,000
6: $50,000
7: $50,000
8: $50,000
9: $50,000
10: $11,500,000,000

The median value is $50,000. (Since we have an even number of data points, we take the mean of the two middle values.)

Now, to calculate the *mode* earnings of all 10 people, you simply count which value occurs the most frequently.

Annual Earnings	Count
$50,000	9
$11,500,000,000	1

This one is pretty simple: the mode earnings are $50,000, as that figure appears 9 times out of 10.

So, the mean is just over $1 billion, but the mean and mode are both $50,000. Which value is the most accurate if you're trying to describe the annual earnings of the typical person in the building? (Hint: don't take the average of the three measures!) In this case, the median or the mode would likely be a better metric. (Although if you want to estimate the impact on income tax revenue, then mean might be the most accurate.)

How do you know which "average" someone is talking about when you're looking at the data? If you assume it's the mean, there's a good chance you'll be right, but the only way to know for sure is to ask.

ONE PIECE OF THE PUZZLE

The average person in Miami is born Hispanic and dies Jewish.

That's a joke, but it shows the potential danger of relying on averages. (While Hispanic births are 60 percent of the total in Miami-Dade county, the county is actually less than 5 percent Jewish.)[14]

The strength of an average is that it takes all the values in your data set and simplifies them down to a single number. This strength, however, is also the great danger of an average. If every data point is exactly the same (picture a row of identical bricks) then an average may, in fact, accurately reflect something about each one. But if your population isn't similar along many key dimensions—and many data sets aren't—then the average will likely obscure data points that are above or below the average, or parts of the data set that look different from the average.

Consider two men. One weighs 150 pounds and one weighs 250 pounds. Their average (mean) weight is 200 pounds. But, does the average tell us something meaningful about how heavy *either* man is? In this context, the average can't appropriately answer the question we care about. The average finish time for the 2015 Boston Marathon was 3:46 (3 hours and 46 minutes), according to statistician Raymond Britt (the publisher of RunTriMedia).[15] But none of the women's age groups (as grouped by Britt) were faster than the overall average. If we care about the performance of women in the marathon, what does this average tell us?

Another way that averages can mislead is that they typically only capture one aspect of the data. For example, an article in *Marie Claire* (Australia) showed six women, all of whom weigh the same—154 pounds (70 kg).[16] But when you look at the women, they all have different body types, and they range in height from under five feet tall to over six feet (145–186 cm). The average weight doesn't capture any of this other data.

Finally, like all of the data concepts we cover in this book, average isn't something that should be considered in isolation. Your average is only as good as the data that supports it. If your sample isn't representative of the full population, if you cherry-picked the data, or if there are other issues with your data, your average may be misleading.

COMPARING THE BIG APPLE TO ORANGES

Here's a great example of how the underlying data can affect the average.

In the U.S., the average salary for a mayor is $62,000.

The average salary for a deputy mayor is $83,000.[17]

How can an average deputy mayor make more than the mayor? Well, any one-stoplight town can have a mayor, often one who isn't paid very much. A study done by the *South Whidbey Record* found that the vast majority of small-town mayors make less than $10,000.[18] When you're computing a national average, these low-paid officials will bring that number down.

A salaried deputy mayor, on the other hand, is a luxury that larger cities are more likely to be able to afford. And big cities offer bigger salaries. In New York City, for example, there are four deputy mayors, each of whom makes more than $200,000.[19]

When you're studying mayors, you're looking at the full expanse of cities and towns. When you're studying deputy mayors, you're looking at a much smaller (and likely higher-paying) group of municipalities. So, if you only looked at cities that had deputy mayors, you'd probably find that the average mayor makes more than the average deputy, for those cities. But by studying a sample that includes both cities with *and* without deputy mayors, we end up with statistics that—at first glance—seem completely nonintuitive.

This is another example of how statistical concepts overlap and affect one another. If you're looking at an average, you are—by definition—studying a specific sample set. If you're comparing averages, and those averages come from different sample sets, the differences in the sample sets may well be manifested in the averages. Remember, an average is only as good as the underlying data.[20]

Speaking of jobs and averages, did you know that you might be earning less money by staying where you are? According to *Forbes*, "Staying employed at the same company for over two years on average is going to make you earn less over your lifetime by about 50% or more."[21]

Why? Because, as *Forbes* explains, the average raise if you stay at a company may only net you a 1 percent increase when you factor in the inflation rate. But employees who leave make an average of 10 to 20 percent more. Factor that in over a few job changes, and suddenly you're talking about a significantly bigger paycheck.

We're not saying you should jump ship. The average simply tells you how the group is doing, and your results may vary. But sometimes an average can give you an idea of what you might expect.

Finally, if you're considering a career in broadcasting, you may want to look at the salaries for a TV news anchor. In 2015, the "average" salary was $83,800, according to a Radio Television Digital News Association/Hofstra University Annual Survey. That's not bad, but if you look at the median, it's only $65,000.[22] There could be a number of explanations for this (including the fact that the maximum salary was an eyebrow-raising $875,000, which could raise the mean significantly without changing the median much, if at all). But imagine you're considering going to school for journalism, and you hear "the average salary for a news anchor is $83,800" versus "the median salary for a news anchor is $65,000." Which is more likely to make you choose that path?

THIS IS ONLY A TEST

An average, in its purest form, treats every data point equally. But that's not always what you want.

Imagine you're an English teacher, and you need to give your students their final grades. Throughout the year, your students have taken three quizzes, one midterm exam, and one final exam.

If you want all of the data to count equally, you can simply add up all of the test scores, divide by five (the number of tests), and give students their final grades. But maybe you think that the final exam should count more than the midterm exam, which should count more than the quizzes.

These types of situations call for a *weighted average*. A weighted average is just what it sounds like: you assign each value a weight based on how important it is compared to the other factors. For example, you might say each of the three quizzes is worth 10 percent of your grade, the midterm is worth 20 percent, and the final exam is worth 50 percent, based on how important each test is in terms of measuring the students' performance. Now, assuming your percentages are thoughtfully applied, this weighted average is going to give you a more accurate representation of each student's work.

Keep in mind that a weighted average may be different than a simple (non-weighted) average because a weighted average—by definition—counts certain data points more heavily. When you're thinking about an average, try to determine if it's a simple average or a weighted average. If it's weighted, ask yourself how it's being weighted, and see which data points count more than others. In our test score example, it's clear that the final exam score will count the most and thus affect the average more, which is (hopefully) the teacher's intent in setting up that specific weighting of assignments. In other contexts, however, weighting may not be so intentional—or so obvious.

AN AVERAGE OF AVERAGES

An average combines data. But what happens when the underlying data has already been combined?

If you follow the news, you've probably seen polls of polls—aka aggregation polls—when media outlets (or other organizations) combine various polls into one easy-to-digest number. The BBC, Real Clear Politics, and others produce these on a regular basis.[23]

Now, you already know that an average is based on its component parts, and that the more alike these parts are, the more closely an average will represent each value. But with a poll of polls, you're taking data that may *look* the same on the surface, but is collected, interpreted, and aggregated in ways that may affect the results. This should raise a ton of questions for a smart consumer of data. For example:

- Are all polls treated equally in the aggregation, or are certain ones given more weight based on their sample size, recency, historical accuracy, or other factors?
- Each individual component poll has a margin of error. How are these margins of error accounted for (if at all) in the aggregation poll? Taking an average doesn't remove all of the underlying uncertainty in the polls.
- What are the differences in the component polls (in terms of survey questions, sample sizes, and other methodology), and how do those differences affect each component poll (and the aggregated data)?

The bottom line? Even though these aggregation polls may (at times) be more accurate than individual polls (according to the Princeton Election Consortium and others), one very high-quality survey may tell us more about where candidates stand than averaging a bunch of surveys of variable quality together.[24]

ONE OF THESE THINGS IS NOT LIKE THE OTHERS

Unless you're dealing with a completely identical data set, where every point has the same value, some of your data points are going to be different from the average.

For example, when we wrote about happiness in the United Kingdom earlier in this chapter, we noted that the U.K. had an average happiness score of 7.3. But different regions scored between 7.0 and 7.9.

Those data points all seem to fit together. They're what you would expect to see when surveying a population.

But sometimes, you have a particular observation that doesn't fit. Maybe the data point is much higher (or lower) than all the other data.

Or maybe it just doesn't fall into the pattern of everything else that you're seeing.

These anomalies are called *outliers*. An NFL player is an outlier. A kid who graduates from college at 14 years of age is an outlier. The worst salesperson in your company, who only sold one-third of what the next worst salesperson sold? Also an outlier.

When you're looking at averages, you need to watch out for outliers, because—as you'll see—their effect on averages can be dramatic. It's like adding cream to your black coffee. It's still 95 percent coffee, but a few drops can change the appearance dramatically.

The tricky part is that there aren't really any hard-and-fast rules when it comes to identifying outliers. Some economists say an outlier is anything that's a certain distance away from the mean, but in practice it's fairly subjective and open to interpretation.[25] That's why statisticians spend so much time looking at data on a case-by-case basis to determine what is—and isn't—an outlier.

So, what causes an outlier? Sometimes, it's simply a mistake. Maybe someone entering data on a spreadsheet transposed a few numbers, and typed in 4.9 instead of 9.4. Perhaps a test tube was contaminated, which is why it shows a much higher level of bacteria than normal. Mistakes happen.

Sometimes an outlier is a red flag for something abnormal. When Mark McGwire hit 70 home runs for the St. Louis Cardinals in 1998, it seemed out of the ordinary. And for anyone not using steroids, it was. A decade later, McGwire admitted using drugs during his record-setting season, confirming the suspicions of fans and statisticians alike.

Finally, as you read (or watch or listen to) the news, keep in mind that many stories are newsworthy precisely because they're about outliers. The same old, same old isn't always as exciting as something that's (far) out of the ordinary.

MAKING A SPLASH

If you pay attention to the Olympics, you may already be familiar with one way in which people try to handle outliers—by simply eliminating them. In diving, gymnastics, and other sports, for example, an athlete's score may be calculated by taking all of the judges' scores for an event, dismissing the highest and lowest scores, and then calculating the mean.

This tactic—known as *mean trimming*—can help avoid having a judge's bias or personal preference affect the outcome. And it's possible that mean trimming could have affected the medal standings in at least one event, according to a paper that looked at the diving scores from the 2000 Olympics.[26]

But does mean trimming—this specific method of dealing with potential outliers—work? Ask yourself, what would happen if there was *more than one* judge who was biased in favor of an athlete? The Olympic system—as it's commonly used—only eliminates the one highest and one lowest value. Or consider the fact that mean trimming treats the highest and lowest values as if they're outliers *regardless of whether they truly are or not.* Is this a fair system?

And then there's the question of whether a high or low score—whether it's an outlier or not—is actually a sign of bias. Yes, nationalistic bias may exist—researchers have found that "most judges gave some type of nationalistic bump to their countrymen without giving a similar bump to non-countrymen."[27] But consider the Chinese diving judge. His average score for Chinese divers at the 2000 Olympics was 1.48 points higher than his average score for non-Chinese divers. Seems like a bias, right? But when the researchers analyzed the data, they actually found that he was "apparently the least biased judge" based on his scores. How is this possible? Because the Chinese judge, it turns out, scored both Chinese *and* non-Chinese divers higher than the other judges, on average. And the Chinese divers were really good; in fact, their average scores were 1.44 points higher than non-Chinese divers. So, when researchers looked at the relative magnitude by which this judge's scores were higher for Chinese divers compared to all other divers, it was actually *less* than the amount (aka magnitude) by which other judges elevated the scores of divers from their home countries relative to all others. Does it make sense, then, to discard his scores in this scenario?

OVAL OFFICE OUTLIERS?

Of course, sometimes outliers aren't mistakes or red flags—they're a perfectly valid part of the data. Consider American history. If you look at how many days each U.S. president served in office, you'll see that most of them served either for 1,460 days or 2,921 days (plus or minus a day), which corresponds to four-year and eight-year terms, respectively. But 44 percent of our presidents served for shorter or longer periods of time, making them outliers according to statistician Robert W. Hayden, PhD, who performed the analysis.[28] Every time a president died in office (therefore not completing the rest of his term) he became an outlier—as did the person who replaced him.

So what do you do with outliers? Do you treat them equally, include them with the rest of the data, and have them skew your average? Do you completely ignore them? Is there a middle ground?

It depends. There are no blanket rules, because each case is different, and it's not always easy to identify an outlier. For example, some parents might think their toddler is an outlier because she's in the 35th percentile for height. Other parents might not care unless their kid was in the 5th percentile. After all, when you're looking at averages, you're going to have some values above average—and some below.[29]

The bottom line is, you need to look at the data and see how much of an impact the outlier has on the question you're trying to answer.

Which leads us to Conwood.

A BILLION-DOLLAR BLIP

It was the largest verdict in the history of antitrust law: $1.05 billion. And it all hinged on outlier data.

Conwood Company—a tobacco manufacturer—was suing another tobacco manufacturer (U.S. Tobacco Company) for hindering Conwood's growth.[30] The data expert for Conwood performed a state-by-state analysis to show the alleged impact of U.S. Tobacco's activities on Conwood's market share.[31]

The problem was that the analysis included Washington, D.C.—an extremely small market, relatively—which meant that even small changes in the amount of product sold by Conwood (perhaps getting stocked in just a few stores) translated into large differences in market share.

When the data was analyzed, it was clear that D.C. didn't act like the 48 states that were measured (Alaska and Hawaii were excluded). It was, as antitrust professor Herbert Hovenkamp called it, a "significant outlier."[32] But rather than omit the outlier data, the expert included it, which skewed the rest of the data and resulted in a conclusion that wasn't supported by the rest of the data. As Hovenkamp said, "the plaintiff's expert had ignored a clear 'outlier' in the data."[33]

If that outlier data had been excluded—as it arguably should have been—then the results would have shown a clear increase in market share for Conwood. Instead, the conclusion—driven by an extreme observation—showed a decrease.

If your conclusions change dramatically by excluding a data point, then that data point is a strong candidate to be an outlier. In a good statistical model, you would expect that you can drop a data point without seeing a substantive difference in the results. It's something to think about when looking for outliers.

ARE YOU BETTER THAN AVERAGE?

The average American:

- Sleeps more than 8.7 hours per day[34]
- Weighs approximately 181 pounds (195.5 pounds for men and 166.2 pounds for women)[35]
- Drinks 20.8 gallons of beer per year[36]
- Drives 13,476 miles per year (hopefully not after drinking all that beer)[37]
- Showers six times a week, but only shampoos four times a week[38]
- Has been at his or her current job 4.6 years[39]

So, are you better than average? Would it surprise you if we told you that 55 percent of Americans think they are smarter than average,[40] most think they are better looking than average,[41] and in a recent study, 93 percent said they were more skillful than the average (median) driver.[42] Perhaps Garrison Keillor had it right in his description of Lake Wobegon where "all the women are strong, all the men are good looking, and all the children are above average."[43]

Statistically, it's impossible for 93 percent of drivers to be better than the median. The median is—by definition—the middle value of your data set. But the study didn't say that 93 percent of American drivers *are* more skillful. It said that 93 percent of them *say* they're more skillful.

What we're likely seeing here is an example of illusory superiority— a type of cognitive bias that explains why most people think they're better than others—hence, better than average.[44]

Why does this matter?

- If you think you're a better than average driver, are you going to use your "skill" to justify speeding or taking other risks?
- If you think you're a better than average gambler, are you going to stick around longer (and bet more) at the poker table?
- If you think you're smarter than average, are you going to apply for jobs that are outside your skill set? (Heads up, guys—men tend to overestimate their intelligence more than women do.)[45]

You can be the best statistician in the world, but if you fall prey to these cognitive biases, they're going to affect your ability to interpret data.

How to Be a Good Consumer of Aggregated Data, Averages, and Outliers

Ready to make better decisions using aggregated data, averages, and outliers? Here are five things you can do starting right now:

1. First of all, **know what a summary statistic is**—and what it isn't. Many people think that because a summary statistic represents a

group of data, it represents *everything* about that data. That's not true. It is one metric, measuring one dimension of a data series. As we saw with red states and blue states, a summary statistic can mask variation in the underlying data.

2. Second, **understand what type of average is being presented—a mean, median, or mode.** Most people think of mean when they hear the word "average," but that's not always the case. These three types of averages are very different. Some can be skewed more easily than others. For example, based on mean, the average person in the world has fewer than two arms (most people have two arms, but some have one or none, which brings the mean down, assuming there are very few people with more than two arms). Make sure you know what you're talking about when someone says "average."

3. Third, **ask "an average of what?"** Because an average combines multiple data points, each one of these points can influence the final result. This is where you can apply everything else you will learn in this book. Is the data representative of the sample? Are you looking at an average of averages, each of which may have its own unique characteristics? These are just a few of the questions to ask.

4. Fourth, **see if all the data is treated equally.** Many averages are actually weighted averages, in which some data is given more weight than other data when calculating the results. For example, some election polls use weighted averages to reflect the true population of voting-age adults. Weighting can be a valid statistical tool if done correctly—but you need to know if, and how, it's happening in order to be a smart consumer of data.

5. Finally, **identify outliers, and understand the impact they can have** on your average. Some outliers are perfectly valid parts of the data set. Other times, it makes sense to exclude extreme examples in order to get a fair answer to the question you're asking. One bad apple can spoil the bunch, as they say. Not every outlier is a bad apple—but an outlier can skew your results in a way you need to be aware of.[46]

4

Are You Smarter Than an iPhone-Using, Radiohead-Loving Republican?

Understanding Correlation Versus Causation

As any self-respecting parent will tell you, there's a lot of pressure to make sure little Susie and Johnny are smarter than their classmates.

That's why we make our kids take gifted assessments, start them in training classes at an early age (contributing to the $54+ billion market worldwide for test preparation, tutoring, and counseling),[1] and enroll them in every type of program imaginable.

It turns out, we could have saved our money (and time). Because we've done the research—and now, we're going to tell you exactly how to make your kid smarter.

Based on the latest data, smarter people:

- Wear glasses (AOL)[2]
- Use an iPhone (CNN)[3]
- Are Republican (Pew Research Center)[4]
- Listen to Radiohead (*Wall Street Journal*)[5]
- Stay up late (*Esquire*)[6]
- Are left-handed (*The New Yorker*)[7]
- Drink more alcohol (*Psychology Today*)[8]

Every single factor here has been cited as a characteristic linked to intelligence. So if you really want a "Proud parent of an honor roll student" bumper sticker for your minivan, apparently all you need to do is get your kids glasses and an iPhone, have them watch a few Ronald Reagan speeches, play some Radiohead, don't let them fall asleep before midnight, turn them into lefties, and start them drinking (once they reach legal age, of course).

Have we lost our minds?

No. We've just read a lot of studies and media reports that seem to draw the wrong conclusion from statistical analyses—specifically, reports and articles that confuse *correlation* with *causation*, and therefore, sometimes unintentionally, mislead the reader about the key takeaways.

It's important to note that there are two issues here: first of all, there are the original scientific studies that sometimes confuse correlation with causation. But what you're more likely to encounter in your everyday life are newspaper articles and other media accounts that misreport the findings from valid scientific studies. We've seen many cases in which a finding is reported in the news as causation, even though the underlying study notes that it is only correlation.

From a statistical perspective, we can find lots of apparent connections between two factors, such as wearing glasses and having a high IQ. These types of connections—when there is some sort of relationship between data—are called *correlations*. But, as we'll explore in this chapter, the mere existence of such a statistical relationship between two factors does not imply that there is actually a meaningful link between them. Correlation does not equal causation. It's actually one of the most common ways that people misinterpret data. But don't worry—in this chapter, we'll take a close look at how and why people mistake correlation for causation, and give you the tools to help you understand which everydata you should really believe.

SMARTPHONES = SMART PEOPLE?

So, back to the smart people analysis. We dug a bit deeper into what the actual studies said, and uncovered some interesting caveats, warnings, and facts that might shed some light on these findings.

Let's start with the iPhone study, which studied the state-by-state level of iPhone usage against the percentage of population with a bachelor's degree (among other factors), and found that "iPhone usage rates were positively correlated with education level."[9]

But all this means is that states with the highest percentage of iPhone users were also the states where a higher percentage of people have bachelor's degrees.[10] It doesn't necessarily mean that you're smarter if you use an iPhone.

A correlation is simply a *bivariate relationship*—a fancy way of saying that there is a relationship between two ("bi") variables ("variate"). And a bivariate relationship doesn't prove that one thing caused the other. Think of it this way: you can observe that two things appear to be related statistically, but that doesn't tell you the answer to any of the questions you might really care about—*why* is there a relationship and *what* does it mean to us as a consumer of data?

There can be many reasons why such observed relationships are not causal. For example, if you look at the claim that people who wear glasses are smarter, what the original study actually describes is an association between having more years of schooling and having a form of myopia (nearsightedness).[11] For a moment, let's assume that having more years of schooling actually does mean you are a smarter person (a big if, and a different issue with the article). The study never says smarter people wear glasses, but rather points to a relationship between spending more time in school and the quality of your eyesight. That's a very big difference. And it's a correlation. The headlines catch your attention by reporting the relationship between eyesight and intellect, but the study comes to a more measured conclusion—which may have a very different implication. For example, it may be that the causation is reversed—more time in school may cause more strain on people's eyes and result in myopia (nearsightedness), which can be corrected with glasses.

What about the idea that smarter people stay up later? Well, according to the original research paper, the lowest IQ group in the study goes to bed, on average, at 11:41 p.m., whereas the highest IQ group goes to bed at 12:29 a.m.[12] This paper runs several statistical analyses, and finds that the higher-IQ individuals go to bed later even accounting for their race, age, gender, marital status, parental status, education, earnings, religion, and their hours worked. In this context, the statistical analysis ostensibly has controlled for far more than just a simple bivariate relationship. But, even so, many statisticians would still not consider this evidence of causation, but of a more sophisticated correlation. Even this analysis still hasn't clearly shown that staying up later causes a higher IQ. Again, the causality could be reversed. In other words, being smart might cause them to stay up later. What if people with higher IQs were simply more likely to stay up late to do their homework and read late into the night? You might see the same statistical relationship, but the cause and effect was actually in the opposite direction.

Bottom line?

If you want your kids to be smart, you don't have to get them glasses—or an iPhone.

Now that we've saved you the cost of a new smartphone, let's move on . . .

SEE WHAT'S MISSING

People don't just want to be smarter. They want to be happier. Healthier. Richer.

That's why you'll see headlines like this, from *Business Insider*: "If Your Commute Lasts More Than 45 Minutes, You Will Probably Get Divorced."[13]

Or this, from EliteDaily.com: "Sleep Naked, Dream Bigger: Why the Secret to a Better Life Is As Simple As Taking It Off."[14]

Or this, from *People*: "Living Near a Starbucks Will Increase Your Home's Value."[15]

We're very happy to live near a Starbucks—but not because it increases our home values, since that's not what the article proves.

We're not going to dispute the data, which claims that houses that were the closest to Starbucks appreciated more than 20 percent during a five-year period, while houses that were just a bit farther away appreciated less than 17 percent.[16] But we are going to question the claim that "it looks like Starbucks itself is driving the increase in home values."[17]

Maybe Starbucks puts its stores in the centers of towns and

villages—and home prices rise faster in those areas. For example, Starbucks chief creative officer and president of Global Innovation and Evolution Fresh Retail (and former director of real estate) Arthur Rubinfeld has written an entire book on how everyday franchisees can learn the lessons of Starbucks with respect to site selection; his secrets include looking for oil stains in the parking lot (a sign that there's lots of traffic).[18]

Maybe a Starbucks location is more likely to have sidewalks, and people like living where there are sidewalks. Maybe every time a Starbucks opens, an Apple Store opens next door—and that's what is driving the rise in real estate prices.

We don't know.

And that's the point.

OMITTED VARIABLES

All of these factors—town centers, sidewalks, Apple Stores—are possible *omitted variables*. An omitted variable is one of the primary reasons why correlation doesn't equal causation.

Remember when we talked about bivariate relationships—relationships between two variables? The problem is that often there are more than two variables. You have a relationship between two variables (also known as *dependence*), but there's actually a third variable that matters as well. That's the omitted variable. (And yes, you can have multiple omitted variables.)

Is Starbucks increasing your home's value? Or is it one of these other factors—any of which could, in theory, impact the price of your home?

It's possible that Starbucks is really making your home worth more. It's also possible that Starbucks could serve as a *proxy* for any of the other factors (sidewalks, etc.). A proxy, in this case, is a factor that you believe is closely related—but not identical—to another factor. For example, IQ tests are a proxy for a person's inherent ability. They don't measure your actual ability, just your ability to perform well on a test that supposedly measures intelligence. Sometimes a proxy is used (intentionally or not) to try to compensate for an omitted variable. A proxy may be better than nothing, but it's certainly not a substitute for the real data.

In the Starbucks example, we know there's a relationship between two variables. But we don't know if there are omitted variables. And you can't know you have isolated any meaningful relationship— confirmation that you've controlled for factors that influence your results—if you have omitted variables. There are armies of empirical economists and statisticians who spend their entire careers worrying about this issue of omitted variables.

Just by asking the simple question—"What else could explain this?"—you can start down the road to finding omitted variables. (It's interesting to note that omitted variables tend to be more of a concern in observed data as opposed to experimental data. In other words, if you're looking at two existing data points—such as a home price and a Starbucks location—you may not be aware of other variables that affect them. But if you're running an experiment—for example, seeing how graduate students respond to incentives in a laboratory setting—you can design the experiment to control for potential omitted variables.)

Finally, as you study correlations, keep in mind that variables can be positively correlated or negatively correlated. Think of this simply as whether two things move together or move in opposite directions. Positive correlation: the presence of Starbucks makes home prices rise. One thing increases, and so does another. A negative correlation works the other way: having too many weeds in your yard makes your home price fall. In this case, when one factor increases, the other decreases. In almost any statistical relationship, we care about the direction. We wouldn't draw the same conclusion about Starbucks and home prices if we found putting a Starbucks in your neighborhood lowered your home value.

Another way we begin to put a correlation to the test is thinking about whether it squares with our economic intuition. For example, if we saw a study that said there's a positive correlation between the number of drug dealers and your home value—in other words, the more drug dealers, the more your home is worth—we'd immediately be suspicious (of the data, and the dealers). Trying to identify the type of correlation may help you determine whether it's truly causation—and what the omitted variables might be.

ARE WE BORING YOU?

As a former professor who has received his fair share of end-of-semester evaluations, John was intrigued by the Gender and Teacher Reviews website from Professor Ben Schmidt. This site allows the user to put in any word, then see how frequently that word appears in Rate My Professor reviews for male and female professors across more than two dozen disciplines. (If you go to benschmidt.org/profGender/# you can check it out for yourself.)

The gender differences are extremely interesting from a data perspective. For example, when we entered the word "boring" into Professor Schmidt's website, we got a graph showing that, in most disciplines, male professors were described as boring more often than female professors. In engineering, female professors were described as "incompetent" slightly more than 18 times per million words of text whereas male professors were described similarly only about 12 times per million words.

But when we attempt to understand differences along a key dimension (such as whether a teacher's gender influences whether or not he or she is rated as "boring"), we need to consider whether the relationship we are observing is capturing the whole story, or whether there are some other confounding factors that could explain what we are observing.

In this example, in order to determine whether students rate professors differently whether they are male or female, we need to make sure we are comparing identical professors along all other meaningful dimensions.

It won't surprise you that a range of factors could go into a student's subjective professor evaluations. Here are a few examples:

- How difficult was the class and subject material?
- Did the student get an A in the class?
- How much homework did the student receive?
- Was the class at a time that college students might not like (such as the 8 a.m. Friday class)?
- How accessible was the professor?
- Was the class an introductory course, a course required for a major, or an elective class?

Now, the fact that a number of factors could ultimately determine student rankings is still not enough to draw a conclusion. *The important question is whether any of these "other factors" vary systematically by gender.* In other words, are the apparent differences in evaluations by gender picking up these other factors?

Take an extreme example: assume in the math department, female professors were always assigned to teach the much harder required calculus class, whereas male professors were assigned to teach the very popular statistics elective. If we observed significantly more negative ratings for female professors, it could be simply driven by the fact that female professors were disproportionately teaching the difficult, less popular class that students were more prone to rank negatively in end-of-course evaluations.

This simple example is not to imply that the differences may not be due to the fact that students rank professors differently depending on gender, but we surely can't tell that from a statistical perspective based on these simple observed differences. More work must be done to determine the exact relationship.

WHY IT MATTERS

If you want to know how data impacts your life, it's not enough to know whether there's a statistical relationship between two variables. The question we really care about is this:

If you're seeing a relationship between two variables, is it a true relationship that has meaning, or is it artificial for some reason?

There are many reasons why a relationship can be artificial, but omitted variables are certainly a common cause. And determining causation has implications in nearly every area of our lives.

- What causes cancer?
- Why are black and Latino students less likely to be identified as "gifted," according to a *Washington Post* article?[19]
- Is it safe to legalize marijuana?

These are just a few of the countless questions that can be answered by identifying all the relevant omitted variables and finding the difference between correlation and causation.

BE LIKE MIKE

Correlation is a powerful tool for marketers and the media, especially when you combine it with our desire to be faster, stronger, smarter, and sexier in every aspect of our lives.

Celebrity endorsements are all about correlation. Consider this:

Michael Jordan wore Nikes.
Michael Jordan could dunk.
If I wear Nikes, I can dunk.

We've personally tested this logic, and we can guarantee that it is not true. Even if you buy every model of sneakers that Michael Jordan ever wore, you're probably not going to get above the rim if you're five-foot-six-inches tall and you never work out.

You're not Michael Jordan. The omitted variables—such as his height and the countless hours of practice he put in—help explain why he won the NBA dunk contest, and you can't.

Just because something worked for a celebrity doesn't mean it will work for you. Assuming that it will is a classic correlation versus causation error.

Another classic mistake?

Jeffrey Brown—an economist and dean of the College of Business at the University of Illinois—offered this example when we interviewed him. "Suppose that every Monday morning, your dog starts barking. A few minutes later, the garbage truck arrives. It would obviously be a mistake to assume that your dog's bark causes the garbage truck to come. In this case, it is likely that the causality is reversed—your dog just hears the garbage truck before you do. Few people would make this exact mistake, and yet they make similar errors in their decision making on a daily basis in other contexts."

Even if you have more data, the problem does not always go away. For example, as Brown noted, you could observe the dog–truck relationship for a decade—but it still does not mean the dog called for the garbage truck. Watch out for these types of reverse causality situations, and make sure you're not inferring causality simply because of the timing of events.

THE BABY, THE BATHWATER, AND THE BORDEAUX

When economist Emily Oster got pregnant, two of the first things she wanted to know (like many moms-to-be) were how much coffee and alcohol she could safely consume.

She didn't want anecdotal advice from friends and neighbors. She didn't want vague advice from her doctor. And she didn't want correlations.

But that's exactly what many recommendations were based on. For example, in examining the link between coffee consumption and higher miscarriage rates, she found numerous differences between women who drink coffee and women who don't drink coffee, "differences that could themselves be responsible for the differences in miscarriage rates."[20]

In other words, she found omitted variables.

Fortunately, as an economist, Oster knew how to understand the numbers. She didn't just listen to her doctors and look at a few articles online. But finding the truth wasn't easy. She ended up going through hundreds of studies to read the original findings for herself, rather than relying on the interpretations of others. (And yes, she had an occasional alcoholic beverage—and drank three to four cups of coffee a day—during her pregnancy.)

Even if you have the training to interpret data correctly—and you're well on your way—you can probably see that it takes significant time and effort to find the truth.

Many economists (those who focus on observations and experiments, rather than simply relying on theory) spend their entire careers assessing and thinking about omitted variable bias, and it's not uncommon for social scientists to spend hundreds of hours analyzing data to prove correlation or causation (or vice versa). We're not trying to deter you—only to let you know the discipline and effort it can take to get to the bottom of things. That said, in our experience, just knowing how and when to question the data will put you way ahead of most people.

WHERE DO YOU RANK?

What if you're truly unable to determine what the omitted variables are?

Here's an example.

If you run a business, you would probably love to nearly double the traffic to your company's website. After all, the number-one spot on Google search results gets almost twice the traffic that the number-two spot does.[21] Depending on your business, moving up just one spot in Google rankings could bring millions of additional visitors.

So how do you improve your ranking?

According to Google, the engine determines search results using algorithms that rely on "more than 200 unique signals or 'clues' that make it possible to guess what you might really be looking for."[22]

The problem is that Google doesn't give you details about what those 200-plus signals are—perhaps because it doesn't want to give away its competitive advantage.

How do you deal with more than 200 omitted variables? Well, if you click over to Moz.com, you'll see charts showing how more than 160 factors correlate to search engine rankings.[23] It's interesting stuff, and probably very useful if you're looking for ways to increase your page ranking.

But it's *not* definitive, because it's based largely on correlations. To its credit, Moz.com uses the word "correlation" 12 times on the page.[24] In a separate blog post, it goes even further, explaining that "correlation data isn't (necessarily) showing us ranking factors."[25]

Sometimes, you simply can't get your hands on the omitted variables. Maybe the data is proprietary. Maybe it was accidentally destroyed, or never recorded in the first place. In these cases, you can try to reverse engineer the data and tease out some correlations. Just keep in mind that—even if you're using the best data that's available to you—it's still an uphill battle to prove causation.

GRILLED CHEESE SEX (OR, THE TITLE WE ALMOST USED FOR THIS BOOK)

Here's another excellent headline from the *Huffington Post:* "Grilled Cheese Lovers Have More Sex and Are Better People, According to Survey."[26] (The only thing better than the title was the website address, which included the text "grilled-cheese-sex-bow-chica-bow-wow.")

We know what you're thinking. Is it true? Does cheddar really make *everything* better?[27]

According to the article, a survey found that 32 percent of people who *like* grilled cheese have sex six or more times each month, while only 27 percent of people who *don't like* grilled cheese have sex that frequently.

Even if we ignore the other flaws in the survey (be wary of self-reported data), it's pretty clear that this is a correlation. There's a relationship between people's love for grilled cheese and their love lives. But there is no evidence that one causes the other. Hence, a correlation—but not causation.

That said—from a purely statistical standpoint—you can't always say that there *isn't* causation just by looking at the data. In this case, there simply isn't enough data to know *what* caused the extra time in the sack. Could it have been all those grilled cheese sandwiches? Sure. Or it could have been a million other variables. Just because you haven't *proven* causation, doesn't mean it *can't* be causation.

And that's how you practice safe statistics.

I SCREAM, YOU SCREAM

Did you know that the amount of sunlight in California correlates with the number of lawyers in American Samoa?[28]

Or that the total amount of revenue generated by bowling alleys in the U.S. correlates to the per capita consumption of sour cream?[29]

These are just a few of the highly entertaining *spurious (aka misleading) correlations* we found on the Spurious Correlations website (tylervigen .com), run by Harvard Law School student Tyler Vigen.[30]

Spurious correlations are useful because they highlight the existence of omitted variables and illustrate the potential danger of equating correlation with causation.

We asked Vigen his opinions about different types of spurious correlations, and how people can do a better job interpreting them. "Take the oft-cited example of the strong correlation between ice cream sales and murder rates," noted Vigen. "Both go up in the summer. The omitted variable is warm weather, which has a documentable effect on crime *and* makes people hungry for ice cream." In this case, the correlation is spurious because another variable (warm weather) exists—it's just omitted when people show the correlation between ice cream sales and murder.

But there is another type of spurious correlation. Consider the correlation between sunlight in California and lawyers in American Samoa. "Here," explains Vigen, "not only is there no obvious connection between the two, but there is *also* no obvious third variable that could be causing both." In these types of situations, "pure probability has taken over; the fact that these two line up is due exclusively to chance. The computer only found it because I fed it thousands of data points to crunch through, but there is no actual connection between the two."

This difference—between omitted variables and unrelated spurious variables—is one of the most interesting but difficult-to-explain aspects of spuriosity, according to Vigen. "Both are examples of spuriosity, but the way they work is decidedly distinct."

Courtney Coile—professor of economics at Wellesley College—agrees, noting that "these 'spurious correlations' are amusing, but ultimately probably less interesting than the cases where we can imagine a reason for the correlation—whether we think it reflects a causal effect of one series on the other or whether the correlation might explained by a third factor."

This is an important difference to keep in mind when you look at correlations in your everyday life. Ask yourself: Is the correlation purely a coincidence? Or is it due to an omitted variable?

Now, as a critical consumer of data, you're probably thinking: "Isn't it possible that there are no coincidences? Could there be an omitted variable that we just don't know about, that somehow explains the connection between sunlight in California and lawyers in American Samoa?"

We're not going to say it's impossible, just like we're not going to say that the Tooth Fairy doesn't exist. You don't ever *really* know that you factored for everything. But you can usually eliminate factors that are clearly ridiculous. (If you think eating grilled cheese sandwiches means you're going to have more sex, you're probably smoking more than Gouda.) Statistics isn't always perfect. But it gives us a framework for evaluating data in a scientific way.

LOST IN TRANSLATION

So why do many people get confused about correlation and causation?

In some cases, the data is simplified, exaggerated, or misrepresented in some way.

Remember the CNN article we talked about earlier: "Smarter people use iPhones—study."

If you only look at the headline, you might assume that there's a correlation between being smart and using an iPhone. But that's *not* what the original article—or study—said. In fact, the article that CNN references never uses the word "smart."[31] Neither does the original white paper that the referenced article is based on.[32]

In this case, the correlation portrayed in the media is not the correlation that was asserted in the original study. To be fair, even though CNN uses the word "smart," the article doesn't explicitly state that using an iPhone makes you smarter. But sometimes correlations are presented in a way that could *imply* a causal relationship—something else you need to watch out for.

As University of Michigan professor of law J. J. Prescott explained, one big mistake most people make is due to "the easy, natural way the mind conflates causation with correlation. In news articles, this is almost always an issue, because stories about associations are just much less compelling than a story about causation. So, journalists (and even scholars) are vague, allowing readers to see what they want to see."

Remember the "dot-com" crash of the early 2000s, when there were deep declines in the stock market—and rising participation of older individuals in the labor force? Dr. Coile—who is also a member of the National Bureau of Economic Research's Economics of Aging Program (which, it should be noted, informs rather than drives policy)—recalls that there were many media stories during this time suggesting that this rise in participation was driven by workers delaying retirement in order to recoup their stock market losses.

"It's easy to notice two phenomena that go together and sound like they might plausibly be related," Coile told us, "but much harder to determine whether the relationship is causal." In fact, when she and a colleague looked into this further, they found "no evidence that groups with more exposure to the stock market (like college-educated workers) were retiring later than other workers during bust years and earlier during boom years." They also found that the number of workers who had enough stock assets for the decline in the market to affect their retirement decision was too small to explain changes in the size of the labor force. In the end, explained Coile, "even though the story sounded plausible, the stock market was less important than other factors in explaining changes in labor force participation during this time."

As you're consuming your everydata, keep in mind that skilled magazine writers, TV producers, and advertising copywriters know how to manipulate words, because their job is to get your attention. Don't fall for it. Read every word. Think about what they're saying—and what they're not saying.

For example, let's say you're a reporter at a magazine. One day, you read about a study that finds a correlation between eating brownies and gaining weight. Your editor asks you to write a story about it, and to give her some headline options. Here are the headlines you suggest:

- "Scientists find link between brownies and weight gain."
- "Lose your gut. Skip the brownies."

- "Brownies—the worst thing you can eat?"
- "Eating brownies tied to weight gain."
- "Do brownies make you fat?"
- "How to lose 20 pounds by skipping the brownies."

None of these headlines actually says that eating brownies causes weight gain. But you can see how they may imply causation, without actually saying that there is a causal relationship.

Sometimes, the best way to uncover the truth is by asking questions. If you see the headline "Eating brownies tied to weight gain" and you simply ask, "*How* is eating brownies tied to weight gain?" the answer should reveal the true relationship between these two variables.

HERE COMES THE SUN

Perhaps another reason that so many people conflate correlation with causation is because of the way we're hardwired to interpret data.

"The human brain is a pattern-recognition machine," explained Ron Friedman in an interview. Friedman is a social psychologist who specializes in human motivation, and the author of *The Best Place to Work: The Art and Science of Creating an Extraordinary Workplace.*

"In the past, before the invention of books or the search engine, uncovering links between cause and effect was essential to our survival," noted Friedman. "Our brains evolved to look for order and find predictability. We can't help it—we look for connections everywhere, and even see them where they don't exist."

Causation is comforting. We want to find it.

"We're programmed to uncover links between events, to interpret coincidences as proof of causality," added Friedman. "When the reason why something happens isn't clear, it's our natural tendency to try and fill in the blanks and attribute cause."

The solution? You can't stop your brain from filling in the blanks. But you can understand how your brain works, and take the extra step to look for proof of causation.

If you're a diehard Boston Red Sox fan and you think they only win games when you wear your lucky t-shirt, you should realize that you're creating a fictional causal relationship based on patterns.[33]

We're pretty sure that lucky jerseys don't make a difference. But it doesn't change the fact that people like having an explanation for things. We like understanding the world around us. Making the leap from correlation to causation gives us that understanding. But that doesn't mean it's the right way to interpret data.

A SHOT IN THE DARK

Consider the debate surrounding the MMR (measles, mumps, and rubella) vaccine and its supposed link to autism. Maybe you heard celebrity mom Jenny McCarthy talk about parents who say their baby got a fever, stopped speaking, and became autistic after being vaccinated.[34]

That's a correlation—not causation.

So why do one-third of parents surveyed believe that vaccinations can cause autism?[35] The journal article widely credited with establishing a link has been retracted.[36] A study of more than 95,000 kids found that "receipt of the MMR vaccine was not associated with increased risk" of autism spectrum disorders.[37]

But what would you do if your child suddenly became withdrawn and stopped talking after she received her measles shot? Wouldn't you wonder if there was a connection? Wouldn't you want to know *why* your child was now on the autism spectrum?

We think you should vaccinate your kids. The science has been clear in dispelling any causal relationship between the MMR vaccine and autism. But you can see how a parent's emotions could affect the way he or she interprets data. Keep this in mind the next time you're debating causation regarding an emotional issue.

This idea of looking for answers is related to *confirmation bias*, which is the tendency to interpret data in a way that reinforces your preconceptions. With confirmation bias, you aren't just looking for *an* answer—you're looking for a *specific* answer.

Confirmation bias can affect nearly every aspect of the way you look at data, from sampling and observation to forecasting—so it's something to keep in mind anytime you're interpreting data. When it comes to correlation versus causation, confirmation bias is one reason that some people ignore omitted variables—because they're making the jump from correlation to causation based on preconceptions, not the actual evidence.

LAST BUT NOT LEAST

Even if you establish causation, remember that all it does is show that one thing caused another. It doesn't tell you about the *impact* or *magnitude* of the results—two topics we'll talk about in chapter 5.

If all you want to know is whether X caused Y, then establishing causation is good enough. But if you want to know how X (and therefore Y) will affect your everyday life, then you need to ask more questions.

So how do you deal with causality and prove definitively that a relationship is causal rather than simply correlation?

We realize that a lot of our advice is telling you what traps to watch out for, and what *not* to do. This book isn't meant to be a statistics textbook. Unfortunately, we don't have the space to teach you how to run a perfect statistical analysis, or determine the exact correlation. But that's okay, because our goal is simply to help you make better decisions by recognizing the difference between correlation and causation, and understanding some of the reasons that people confuse the two—so you can avoid making the same mistakes.

How to Be a Good Consumer of Correlation and Causation

So now, armed with a better understanding of the distinction between correlation and causation, here are some steps to keep in mind when consuming data about a statistical relationship:

1. Ask yourself **what is being represented in the news article or research**. Does the story actually use the phrase "causal" relationship?

More often than not, a headline or article might appear to be *implying* causality, but if you actually dig deeper, you will find most of the actual research is only a discussion of some type of correlation.

2. In understanding any statistical analysis, step back and **apply common sense**—does the relationship actually make intuitive sense? Why should grilled cheese improve your sex life? Does it make sense that smarter people use iPhones? Although statistics can often illuminate unexpected surprises, try not to view things in a vacuum, separate from your own intuition.

3. If you are presented with a relationship between two things, **ask yourself: Could something else be driving what I observe here?** Are there other omitted factors that could *actually* be the important factors in understanding this relationship?

4. **Be on the lookout for reverse causality.** Finding a statistical correlation doesn't necessarily mean that things go in one direction. Do smart people stay up later? Or do people stay up later because they're smart? Don't discount the possibility of a feedback loop, where X affects Y and Y affects X at the same time (e.g., smart people stay up later, which gives them more time to get smart, which makes them stay up later...).

5. Finally, for a scientist, **it is actually a high bar to prove a causal relationship**. Be wary of relationships that are attributed to causality, especially in light of potential omitted variables.

5

In Statistics We Trust

Is What You're Seeing True?

Even in Washington, D.C.—a city filled with awe-inspiring monuments—the Vietnam Veterans Memorial Wall stands out. Dozens of black granite panels are inscribed with the names of those killed or missing in action—more than 58,000 total.

But is it possible some servicemen died (and some lived) instead of others because a process that was supposed to be random . . . wasn't?[1]

In 1969, the United States had half a million troops in Vietnam. The Selective Service System began preparations for the first draft lottery since World War II to determine which men would be inducted the following year. A random drawing would take place on December 1, 1969, and approximately 850,000 young men who were classified as "draft eligible" would be assigned a draft number based on their birthday.

Here's how it worked: officials put 366 blue plastic capsules in a box; each capsule contained a date from January 1 to December 31.[2] The contents of the box were poured into a large glass container, and officials pulled capsules one at a time out of the glass container.

If your birthday was the date inside the first capsule picked (September 14), you were assigned number one. If your birthday was in the second capsule (April 24), you were assigned number two. And so on. The lower the number, the sooner you would be inducted. It was expected that if your number was in the top third of those pulled, you would likely be on your way to boot camp—and then on to Vietnam—in the near future.

In theory, this system was supposed to be random. Every man would have the same chance of having his birthday picked first. But in actuality, it wasn't.

"Statisticians Charge Draft Lottery Was Not Random," read the headline in the *New York Times* on January 3, 1970.[3] According to the article, men whose birthdays were in December were more likely to have received a low draft number than those whose birthdays were in January. In fact, as a graph in the *Times* demonstrated, the average draft number was more than 200 for the months of January through May, then declined steadily every subsequent month except for one (October), ending with 122 in December.

In this chapter, we are going to explore different ways that scientists try to determine whether a statistical effect is due to random chance.

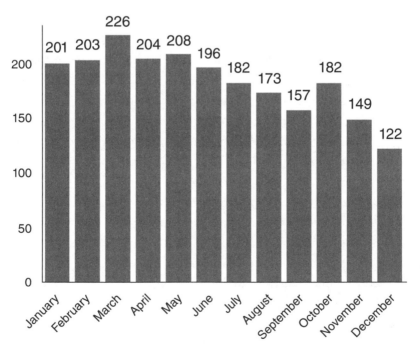

Average lottery number for those born in each month

FIGURE 5-1

In this case, the probability that this pattern occurred by chance was 50,000 to 1, according to statisticians interviewed by the *Times*.

So if it wasn't chance, what explains the pattern?

From a statistical point of view, there is one specific scenario in which you'd *expect* the later months to have average lower numbers (picked sooner). That scenario? *If capsules from later months were at the top of the jar, rather than mixed randomly throughout.*

The chief of public information for the Selective Service System explained to the *Times* how the capsules were mixed. First, the men filled 31 capsules with the January dates. "The January capsules were then placed in a large, square wooden box and pushed to one side with a cardboard divider, leaving part of the box empty."[4] Then, they added the February capsules to the empty side of the box, and used the divider to push them over. This happened with each subsequent month. With this process, the January capsules were mixed with others 11 times (as were the February capsules, since January and February were the first two groups mixed together—a fact the *New York Times* article appears to have mistaken), then the March capsules were mixed with others 10 times, April 9 times, and so on.

The capsules containing the December dates were mixed with the others only once.

The Selective Service System had its reasons for conducting the lottery this way—perhaps including the fact that back in the 1940s some capsules had broken open when officials had tried to stir them using a wooden paddle (made from "a fragment of wooden rafter from Independence Hall in Philadelphia," according to a *Science* article).[5]

It's not clear—at least from a historical account—how the capsules were poured from the box into the glass jar. But surely you can see how a method of adding and mixing capsules one month at a time could lead to differences. Ask yourself—would we have seen the opposite results had the capsules been poured into the glass jar from the other end of the box in which they were mixed?[6]

In this example, the lottery numbers were supposed to be "randomly" drawn; as a result, there was a baseline pattern we would expect to see if the numbers were truly drawn with equal probability. Statistically, by showing they could not fit this pattern, it was clear the pattern of birthday numbers was unlikely the result of a truly random process. (Although using birth dates—if done correctly—could be a random way to approach the problem.)

To be a sound consumer of everydata, you need to determine how likely it is that the relationships you are seeing in the data are true. Are the relationships you're seeing in the data due to random chance, or is there something else going on? How sure are you that you're seeing something real—and how accurately and precisely can you measure that effect? These are a few of the questions we'll explore in this chapter.

POLL POSITION

In the summer of 2015, a *Bloomberg Politics* poll asked Republicans who their first choice would be for president of the United States.

Ten percent of the people chose Jeb Bush. Eight percent chose Scott Walker. Which means that Bush led Walker by just 2 percent.[7]

Maybe.

Because when you look at the data, it's possible that Bush was actually *losing* by 6 percent. It's also possible Bush was up by more than 10 percent.

How? The *Bloomberg* poll had a *margin of error* of ± 4.4 percent.[8]

Inherent in any poll of "likely voters" is the randomness induced by the sample of people who were surveyed. Margin of error is one common way to measure statistical uncertainty from such polling. It's a way of answering the question, How sure are you?

Many people misinterpret margin of error, and think it means that the candidate's level of support is definitely within this range. That's not quite true.

What the margin of error actually means, as Bloomberg explains, is that "if this survey were repeated using the same questions and the same methodology, 19 times out of 20 the findings would not vary from the percentages shown here by more than plus or minus 4.4 percentage points."[9]

So, back to the *Bloomberg* poll—why wouldn't we see the same results 20 out of 20 times? And why is there such a wide range—plus or minus 4.4 percent?

Because polling is taking a sample. In this case, it's a sample of 500 people. And a sample is not the full population—consider that more than 60 *million* people voted Republican in the last presidential election. In this context, with a sample and population of that size, you definitely need to account for sampling error, which we talk about more later in this chapter.[10]

What this means is that Bush may—or may not—actually have led over Walker at the time of this poll. It's hard to tell with this data, given the margin of error. Our best interpretation from the poll is that Bush is ahead. But, with a margin of error of this size, we aren't certain of this fact.

And finally, here's your fun fact of the day: according to the National Bureau of Economic Research, "The introduction of Fox News had a small but statistically significant effect on the vote share in Presidential elections between 1996 and 2000."[11]

BLOWING SMOKE

On the National Cancer Institute's website, there's a page dedicated to sharing information about secondhand smoke and cancer.[12] The fourth question down seems pretty straightforward: "Does exposure to secondhand smoke cause cancer?"

The answer? "Yes."

The National Cancer Institute, which says it offers information that is "science-based, authoritative, and up-to-date,"[13] goes on to list multiple sources that have classified secondhand smoke as a cancer-causing agent.

It says that "inhaling secondhand smoke causes lung cancer in nonsmoking adults."

It states that living with a smoker "increases a nonsmoker's chances of developing lung cancer by 20 to 30 percent."

It even cites the number of adult nonsmokers in the U.S. who die from lung cancer each year due to secondhand smoke—approximately 3,000.[14]

So imagine our surprise when we read an article in the *Journal of the*

National Cancer Institute with the headline, "No Clear Link Between Passive Smoking and Lung Cancer."[15]

Uh, now what? We have the National Cancer Institute and its decades of research, claiming that secondhand smoke *does* cause lung cancer. And we have this study, saying that there is *not* a clear link.

How are you supposed to interpret this data?

You could spend days (if not weeks or months) reading all of the referenced literature from the National Cancer Institute, including a 727-page report from the U.S. surgeon general, and try and figure it all out for yourself.

You could listen to one of the senior investigators on the new study, who said, "We think the message is, this analysis doesn't tell us what the risk is, or even if there is a risk."

Or you could stop and think about how researchers and scientists determine whether their findings are credible.

So what should a smart consumer of data do?

SIGNIFICANT OTHERS

In the movie *Thank You for Smoking*, Aaron Eckhart's character (a spokesperson for the tobacco industry) tells his son, "When you argue correctly, you're never wrong."[16]

It's a line from a lobbyist in a Hollywood satire—but it's an interesting quote to keep in mind as we talk about statistical significance, given that many people feel it's the "correct" way to talk about data.

Statistical significance is a concept used by scientists and researchers to set an objective standard that can be used to determine whether or not a particular relationship "statistically" exists in the data. Scientists test for statistical significance to distinguish between whether an observed effect is present in the data (given a high degree of probability), or just due to chance. It is important to note that finding a statistically significant relationship tells us nothing about whether a relationship is a simple correlation or a causal one, and it also can't tell us anything about whether some omitted factor is driving the result.

Statistical significance refers to the *probability* that something is true. It's a measure of how probable it is that the effect we're seeing is real (rather than due to chance occurrence), which is why it's typically measured with a *p-value*. P, in this case, stands for probability. If you accept p-values as a measure of statistical significance, then the lower your p-value is, the less likely it is that the results you're seeing are due to chance alone.[17]

One oft-accepted measure of statistical significance is a p-value of less than .05 (which equates to 5 percent probability). The widespread use of this threshold goes back to the 1920s, when it was popularized by Ronald Fisher, a mathematician who studied the effect of fertilizer on crops, among other things.[18]

Now, we're not here to debate *whether* a p-value of .05 is an appropriate standard for statistical significance, or even whether p-values themselves are the right way to determine statistical significance.[19]

Instead, we're here to tell you that p-values—including the .05 threshold—*are* the standard in many applications.

And *that's* why they matter to you.

Because when you see an article about the latest scientific discovery, it's quite likely that it has only been accepted by the scientific community—and reported by the media—because it has a p-value below .05.

It may seem somewhat arbitrary, but, as Derek Daniels, PhD (an associate professor at the University at Buffalo) told us, "having a line allows us to stay objective. If there's no line, then we make a big deal out of a p-value of 0.06 when it helps us, and we ignore a p-value of 0.04 when it hurts us."[20]

TAKE A DEEP BREATH

Now let's go back to the secondhand smoke study, and see what the research actually said—that passive smoking "did not statistically significantly increase lung cancer risk."

But, as the researchers on the "no clear link" study pointed out, they were basing some of their conclusions on a relatively small number of people. Out of more than 76,000 women in the study, only 152 of them had never smoked *and* got lung cancer. Is that an issue? Possibly.

Is the fact that they only studied women a concern? Maybe.

What about the fact that they only measured years of exposure to secondhand smoke, rather than intensity (pack years)? After all, you might expect to see a difference in a nonsmoking wife whose husband only smoked on the porch, versus a nonsmoking wife whose husband smoked inside their apartment.

Yes, it's possible that all of these factors matter. But the bottom line is that the study, for the most part, could not show any relationship statistically between secondhand smoke and cancer.[21] That does *not* mean there is no relationship. But it *does* mean that the researchers couldn't distinguish it from pure random chance based on research conventions.

Finally, as we're talking about statistical significance, while there may be some statistical rationales for having the p-value threshold at .05 (including some theories on standard deviations and other measures), having a strict dividing line leads to some consternation for those who don't quite make the cut. In fact, one blogger published a list of 509 "linguistically interesting" ways that results close to statistical significance (but not quite there) were described in peer-reviewed journals.[22] Some of our favorites included:

- "at the cusp of significance"
- "flirting with conventional levels of significance"
- "only a little short of significance"
- "quasi-significant"
- "remarkably close to significance" (p=0.05009 in this case)
- "teetering on the brink of significance"

And with that, we move on.

(SAMPLE) SIZE MATTERS

In a study covered by the *New Yorker* and others, a team of researchers did a series of experiments to see if people are more likely to buy things when they're hungry.[23]

How did they study this phenomenon? In one of their tests, they surveyed 81 shoppers leaving a department store. Now, we've been in checkout lines where it seemed like there were more than 81 people, so we're pretty sure that's not the full population of shoppers on this planet. Which leads us to a key factor in determining statistical significance—sampling.

As you'll recall from chapter 2, sampling lets us estimate the results from the full population. It would be impossible, for example, to ask every single person in the United States who he or she is going to vote for in the presidential election. You'd be on the phone for a *really* long time. So instead, pollsters look at a *sample* of the population.

But sampling isn't perfect.

One of the issues with sampling, as we explored in chapter 2, is that you may be looking at the wrong data for the problem you want to solve. Remember the *Challenger* disaster? The team looked at launch temperatures for a sample of all past flights—only those with O-ring incidents—when they should have been looking at *all* shuttle flights.

But now, let's assume you're looking at the right data, and consider another really important question: Does the sample tell you anything *statistically* about the population? In other words, how sure can you be that your sample is an accurate representation of the rest of the data—the full population?

The simple answer is that there's almost always going to be some measure of uncertainty when you're looking at a sample. In statistical terms, we call this *sampling error*, and it's a way to determine *how much* uncertainty is associated with your sample. Sampling error occurs because not all samples are the same. Even if you take two samples of the same exact size, from the same exact population, you may still get different answers. Think about picking five random M&M's from a bowl filled with M&M's, putting them back, and then picking another five M&M's. How likely is it that you'll get the same colors each time?

Researchers spend a fair amount of time assessing the *power* of their studies—which simply means the extent to which the size of the sample relates to the ability to tease out statistical effects. For your purposes as an everyday consumer of data, just be aware that sample sizes (the number of data points a particular finding was based on) can make a big difference in terms of whether or not findings are statistically significant.

HOW SURE ARE YOU?

Remember margin of error as one way we express statistical confidence in a poll? There is a similar (but slightly different) tool used to measure our level of statistical certainty about the results from scientific studies, called a *confidence interval*. This metric is typically expressed as a range of values, rather than the ± you see with margin of error. But they function the same way, by telling you the range of values within which you're likely to see the estimate (assuming, of course, you have a random sample).

Just like the margin of error, the wider the interval, the more likely the interval contains the true value (for the entire population). Think of it this way: if Bush is polling at 10 percent, it's quite likely that his actual level of support is somewhere between 5 percent and 15 percent. It's less likely—statistically speaking—that his actual level of support is in a narrower range, such as 8 to 12 percent.

And that brings us to *confidence level*—the term we use to determine *how* confident we are that we're measuring the data correctly. The confidence level is typically shown as a percentage, and it tells you what percent of the samples would include the true value.

Confidence intervals and levels are commonly used in scientific papers and studies. But you rarely see them in media reports of those papers and studies. And this is an issue because when you don't have confidence levels and intervals, you don't have the full story.

For example, an NPR story said people who drink a sugar-sweetened beverage each day "had an 18 percent increased risk of developing [diabetes] over a decade."[24] It's true that is what the study said. But if you read the original document, you'll see that the 18 percent figure has a "95% confidence interval 8.8% to 28%."[25] So while it's certainly *possible* that the increased risk is 18 percent, a more accurate interpretation might be that it's highly probable the risk is between 8.8 and 28 percent.

Confidence intervals require the consumer to have a nuanced understanding of the underlying data, and this may get lost as data is reported by the media. We're not trying to pick on NPR or CNN or anyone in the media, because—as much as it breaks our data-loving hearts—most people don't care about all the nitty-gritty details. And that's okay. You don't have to know every confidence interval of every study you read about. But you should know that they exist, what they mean, and how they influence the data you consume every day. Or, in the words of Donald Rumsfeld, you want to distinguish between "unknown unknowns" and "known unknowns."[26]

Of course, media interpretation of data is a different issue from original scientific studies that may have false findings. In a paper titled "Why Most Published Research Findings Are False," John Ioannidis wrote, "There is increasing concern that in modern research, false findings may be the majority or even the vast majority of published research claims."[27]

As *Science News* put it, "if you believe what you read in the scientific literature, you shouldn't believe what you read in the scientific literature."[28]

We're not sure about Ioannidis's claims about the "majority" of published claims being false, but we've certainly seen dozens—if not hundreds—of published studies that had notable concerns regarding statistical significance. It is not at all uncommon for a published study to have findings that are simply not supported by the data.

SPILLING THE BEANS

If you read *Medical News Today,* you may have seen this headline: "Study links coffee intake with reduced risk of endometrial cancer."[29]

The article explained what endometrial cancer is (you may know it as uterine cancer), told readers about the study, and relayed the findings—that drinking approximately four cups of coffee a day can reduce a woman's risk of getting endometrial cancer.

And then, we come to the sixth paragraph: "The women completed dietary questionnaires, and the researchers assessed the link between 84 foods and nutrients consumed and the risk of endometrial cancer."[30]

So, the researchers studied 84 different things, and found that one of them reduces cancer.[31]

Statistical significance, as you'll recall, is often based on the probability of finding results. So it follows that the more things you study, the more likely it is that you're going to "discover" one of them is—ta-da!—statistically significant. Statisticians call this the multiple comparison problem. If you are testing for a relationship and determining statistical significance with a standard of 95 percent certainty, then there is a 98.7 percent chance you will find at least one positive result among 84 tests *purely by random chance.*

Coffee is one of the most-studied foods on the planet. In fact, a Vocativ.com article titled "We Give Up. Let's Just Say Coffee Cures Everything" found "about 2,000 papers that refer to coffee as some kind of preventative potion."[32]

Two. Thousand. Papers.

Written about a drink that contains more than 1,000 chemicals.

Honestly, we'd be more surprised if a study didn't find some benefit from drinking coffee.

That said, remember this advice from economist J. J. Prescott: the lack of evidence for an effect (i.e., failure to reject the null, for you stat geeks) is *not* the same thing as evidence of a lack of an effect (i.e., accepting the null). In other words, just because you don't have proof that something happens doesn't mean it didn't happen. Even if you don't hear (or see) a tree fall in the woods, it still could be on the ground.

YOU SAY TOMATO

In today's world, it's pretty easy to find published studies that support opposite sides of an argument. Secondhand smoke does—and doesn't—cause lung cancer. Same with wine. Milk and eggs, tomatoes and potatoes, coffee and even corn . . . the list of foods that cause (and prevent!) cancer, depending on which study you read, goes on and on.

In fact, two researchers decided to explore this exact phenomenon, in a paper titled "Is everything we eat associated with cancer? A systematic cookbook review."

They started by picking 50 ingredients from cookbook recipes, then did some research and found that 40 out of those 50 "had articles reporting on their cancer risk."[33]

While some of those articles reported an association with a higher cancer risk, other articles noted that these same foods might actually help protect against cancer.

So how do you decide what to eat for dinner?

Statistical significance can be a powerful tool, when used correctly. Justin Wolfers is an economist who is a fellow at the Brookings Institution, a professor at the University of Michigan, and a regular columnist for the *New York Times* on economics issues. We asked him what a reader should do when confronted with so many conflicting studies. "Generally speaking," he explained, "no single study ever overturns a pre-existing literature. Accretions to knowledge are typically a bit more gradual than that."

Remember this the next time you are confronted with the latest study that appears to have overturned years of research; it may be interesting and even true, but should be viewed in the context of all of the other work that has been done as well in an area. Just because there's a statistically significant study that says X prevents cancer, doesn't mean there isn't another study that says X doesn't prevent cancer.

SOUND EFFECTS

Let's say you work for a pharmaceutical company, and one of your products is a drug that extends the life of people with ALS (Lou Gehrig's disease). You've run studies that confirm there is, in fact, a statistically significant effect. The drug works.

Now, the key question is *how well* does it work? Will it extend someone's life by a day? A month? A year?

In statistical terms, this is called *magnitude*. Essentially, magnitude is the size of the effect. It's a way to determine if the results are meaningful. Without magnitude, it's hard to get a sense of *how much* something matters. Consider these two statements:

Drinking coffee lowers your risk of cancer.
Drinking coffee lowers your risk of cancer by 18 percent.

The 18 percent is the magnitude—it's the *difference* that coffee can have (according to this study).

The size of the effect is different from whether or not it's statistically significant. Just because something is statistically significant doesn't mean it's a huge effect—or a tiny one, for that matter.

That said, it's important to remember that the magnitude of an effect can change, depending on the relationship. For example, you might agree with the blanket statement that water is good for you. But *how* good it is for you varies depending on how much you consume. Dr. Oster, writing for *FiveThirtyEight* (and citing a study from the *American Journal of Epidemiology*), found that "drinking more water lowered the risk of dying."[34] Both women and men could lower their risk by having three or more cups a day. But if you drink *too much* water in a day, you can die.

Think about magnitude when you look at results. For example, when you read a study that says "coffee prevents endometrial cancer," it's important to see at what level. Do you only have to drink one cup to reap the benefits? Or do you have to drink four cups?

DOES IT MATTER?

Even if you have a study that's statistically significant, even if it has a large effect, if you're talking about consuming data in your everyday life, one of the most important questions you can ask is, "How will this affect my life?" Take our coffee example. What are the "benefits" of that extra cup of coffee for your cancer risk? Does drinking more java reduce your risk by .00001 percent or 10 percent?

Answering that question highlights the difference between statistical impact and economic impact.

Statistical impact is simply saying that yes, there is a relationship of some undetermined size.

But most people don't make decisions based on statistical associations. Instead, we look at the economic impact—How much is this decision going to cost us in terms of our time, our money, our health, or other resources?

We asked Dr. Oster (who decided to eat deli meat during her pregnancy despite a slight risk of listeria) about magnitude, statistical versus economic impact, and the difference between what researchers focus on and what the general public should be concerned about.

"I think the way I would put it," she said, "is that there is a difference between the theoretical risk and risks that are large enough to be concerned about. In this case of listeria—it is true that there are cases of listeria in deli meat, but there are also cases in spinach and cantaloupe and ice cream. So you can definitely decrease your risk an infinitesimal amount by not having deli meats—which makes sense for some people and some set of preferences—but the decrease is small."

Statistical significance matters.

But in many cases—for everyday life—the magnitude and economic impact matters most of all.

BUT WAIT, THERE'S MORE

Statistical significance is not the one thing to rule them all. Even if you've established statistical significance, you still have to watch out for everything else we've talked about in this book (omitted variables, outliers, etc.), not to mention a whole host of biases (confirmation, selection, etc.).

Consider:

- In the endometrial cancer study, the researchers "found a link, but not a cause-and-effect relationship, between coffee drinking and lower risk of endometrial cancer," according to WebMD.[35] In other words, *there was correlation, but not causation.*
- "P-hacking" (named after p-values) is a term used when researchers "collect or select data or statistical analyses until nonsignificant results become significant," according to a *PLoS Biology* article."[36] This is similar to *cherry picking*, as p-hacking researchers simply throw things at the wall until something sticks, metaphorically speaking (although there probably are some scientists who actually throw things at the wall until something sticks . . .).

- A fascinating *New Yorker* article (is there any other kind?) examines *publication bias* as a possible cause of the "decline effect," in which the size of a statistically significant effect declines over time. Why? One statistician found that "ninety-seven per cent of all published psychological studies with statistically significant data found the effect they were looking for," making it perhaps less likely that future studies would be able to replicate these results.[37]

- *The Journal of Epidemiology and Community Health* published a paper finding no evidence that reduced street lighting at night increased traffic collisions or crime in England and Wales. But the authors (rightfully) acknowledged the possibility of *selection bias*—they didn't get data from approximately one-third of the local authorities, and said, "It is possible that local authorities may have declined to participate because of expected or known increases in collisions or crime in their areas due to lighting changes."[38]

Just because something is statistically significant doesn't make all the other issues go away.

How to Be a Good Consumer of Data by Knowing If What You're Seeing Matters

Just because you're surrounded by data doesn't mean you should use that data to make decisions about your life. Here are five things you can do right now to understand whether the data you're seeing actually matters.

1. Start by **asking if a result could be due to random chance.** Being a sound consumer of data frequently requires you to rule out that things you are observing are due to random chance. You might talk with five guys who all love hamburgers, but the sample size is likely too small to know what percentage of *all* guys love hamburgers. Maybe

you just found the only five guys in the world who love them. In many cases, determining whether the results are random or not requires having some baseline against which to compare a result you find.

2. Understand that **many findings are actually based on probability**. A "statistically significant" finding, as the term is commonly applied, simply means that it is 95 percent likely for the result to be within confidence intervals. A closer look at a p-value can tell you *how* probable it is that the results are not simply due to random chance—and oftentimes that's as close as we can come to certainty—but keep in mind that we're still just measuring probability.

3. **Know that the data you see in headlines is often part of a range**. Whether it's expressed as a margin of error (plus/minus in polls) or a confidence interval, often a reported finding is simply an estimate of a value within a given range. When a newspaper article reports that your favorite political candidate is polling at 42 percent, the true range is likely plus or minus a few percentage points. When a scientific study finds that the aptly named MIND diet (featuring fish, berries, and greens) may reduce the progression of Alzheimer's disease, a confidence interval provides the expected range of the effect.

4. Even if the effect is statistically significant, **look at the size of the effect**. If you go swimming in the ocean, you might get attacked by a shark. But it's a very small risk. You're actually "three times more likely to drown at the beach than die from a shark attack," according to a Discovery.com article, citing the University of Florida's International Shark Attack File.[39] It's easy to get worked up about the latest food that's bad for you, or other risks you might face—which is why it's important to think about how large the effect truly is.

5. **Consider the impact** the data has on your life. If you live in Nebraska and never plan on going to the ocean, you don't need to worry about shark attacks, no matter how probable they are. (Unless you're worried about a Sharknado, of course.)[40] If you live in Africa,

you should probably be much more concerned with hippopotamuses, which kill hundreds of people each year (compared with fewer than a dozen people killed annually by sharks), according to the Gates Foundation.[41] Just because a finding has statistical impact—even with a large magnitude—doesn't mean it has an economic impact on your everyday life.

6

Shrinking Africa

Misrepresentation and Misinterpretation

In 1544, Gerardus Mercator was an up-and-coming mapmaker who was sentenced to prison for being a heretic. Apparently, his letters and travels raised the suspicions of local authorities, who didn't approve of his Protestant sympathies.

While many of his contemporaries were beheaded, burned at the stake, or buried alive for their supposed crimes, Mercator was released from prison after seven months, and went on to become the leading European cartographer of his time.

You've probably heard of Mercator. If not, you've almost certainly seen his work, perhaps hanging next to the chalkboard in your elementary school classroom. Most notably, he produced the Mercator world map of 1569—or, as he rather ambitiously titled it, "New and more complete representation of the terrestrial globe properly adapted for use in navigation." (Mercator was not a subtle guy.)

Mercator's new map was specifically designed to do one thing: help sailors chart more accurate routes. It did this by using straight lines to represent the path a ship could take without changing course—a novel approach that made it much easier for ship captains to deliver their goods.

This mapmaking technique required some finagling on Mercator's part, since a sailor's direct path on a three-dimensional globe doesn't automatically translate to a straight line on a two-dimensional map. But Mercator figured out how to do it, and enjoyed the fame and fortune that followed.[1]

FIGURE 6-1 A Mercator projection. Licensed under the Creative Commons Attribution-Share Alike 3.0 Unported license. Created by user $200inaire on Wikimedia Commons. (https://commons.wikimedia.org/wiki/File:Mercator_Blank_Map _World.png#filelinks)

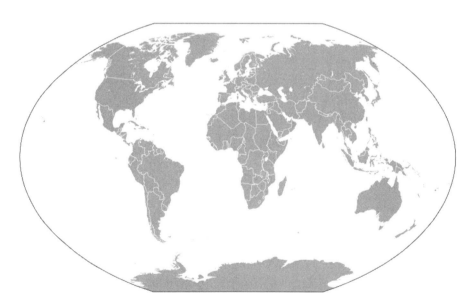

FIGURE 6-2 For comparison purposes, here's a Winkel tripel projection. Licensed under the Creative Commons Attribution-Share Alike 3.0 Unported license. Created by user Hellerick on Wikimedia Commons. (https://commons.wikimedia.org/wiki/ File:1937_world_map_%28Winkel_tripel_projection%29.svg)

Unfortunately, while the new map helped ocean-faring navigators, it also drastically *misrepresented* the size of countries and continents around the globe. Sailors got their straight lines for navigation at great expense, as Mercator's map distorted the size of nearly everything on it. Even worse, the distortion wasn't equal; the farther an object is from the equator, the more distorted it appears.

In practical terms, this means that objects closer to the poles appear to be much larger, relatively speaking, than objects closer to the equator. This artifact is commonly known (to cartographers, at least) as "the Greenland problem" because, on a Mercator map, it looks like Greenland is about the same size as Africa. But it's not. In fact, it's not even close.

If you compare the two based on land area, Africa is approximately *14 times larger* than Greenland. But Africa is on the equator (hence, less distortion) while Greenland sits largely above the Arctic Circle, and therefore looks much larger on a Mercator map than it really is.[2]

So what's the problem? Well, besides a few generations of confused schoolchildren, our concern is that the size (and perceived size) of an object has real implications in the real world. By minimizing Africa's true size, the Mercator map—intentionally or not—influences how people think about the continent geographically, historically, politically...you get the idea. Whether you're planning a vacation, waging a war, or simply debating the importance of Europe versus Africa, the size of a land mass matters.

The problem certainly isn't unique to Mercator maps—translating three-dimensional data to a two-dimensional medium typically requires trade-offs—that's one reason why there are more than 60 commonly recognized types of map projections.[3] But the Mercator map is a perfect example of misrepresented data found all around us.

As you'll see throughout this chapter, misrepresentation of data can be found in nearly every aspect of your life. Whether you're reading an annual report or ordering a burger, you can make smarter decisions if you know some of the many ways in which data is misrepresented and misunderstood.

NO GUESSING

Of course, if you're going to use data to estimate the effectiveness of people, you should probably make sure the data is real. As in, actually real. Not made up. Not a guess. Not even a guesstimate.

Alas, that wasn't exactly the case in *Vergara v. California*, in which the courts found that California's teacher tenure laws burden poor and minority students with ineffective teachers.[4] The case centered around predictions, including whether students' test scores could determine teacher effectiveness, and how a teacher's effectiveness would impact his or her students.

In his ruling, Los Angeles Superior Court Judge Rolf Treu wrote: "Dr. Berliner, an expert called by State Defendants, testified that 1-3% of teachers in California are grossly ineffective."[5]

One to 3 percent seems like a lot. But where did that figure come from?

"I pulled that out of the air," said Dr. David Berliner, the state's expert witness, quoted in a you-have-to-read-it-to-believe-it article on *Slate*.[6] "There's no data on that," he added. The number was simply an estimate, based on Berliner's visits to "lots and lots of classrooms."

Based on Berliner's account in the *Slate* article, he claimed the 1 to 3 percent was an estimate. And he appears to be a respected author, member of the National Academy of Education, and professor emeritus at Arizona State University (go Sun Devils!).[7]

We're strong supporters of education and equal rights. (John chairs the board of directors for Appleseed, a national nonprofit organization that advocates for justice.)[8] We're not arguing the verdict, the outcome, or Berliner's credentials. But, in our opinion, these types of claims should be based on hard data—or noted otherwise.[9]

Perhaps if this one had been, it wouldn't have appeared as implied fact in the judge's ruling.

Maybe the judge would have ruled differently.

And perhaps a case that affects 275,000 teachers and six million students would have had a different outcome.

RAISING THE BAR (CHART)

A good chart can tell a story about the data, helping you understand relationships among data so you can make better decisions. The wrong chart can make a royal mess out of even the best data set.

Let's say we want to figure out the relationship between how many hours of exercise we get per week and how long we can extend our lives. To do so, we'll use data from a study that tracked participants' weekly exercise levels, and how that affected their mortality over time.[10]

Hours of Exercise per Week	Reduction in Mortality Risk
0	0 percent
0–7.5	20 percent
7.5–15	31 percent
15–22.5	37 percent
22.5–40	39 percent
40–75	39 percent
>75	31 percent

As you can see, mortality risk declines by 20 percent when exercise is increased from no exercise up to 0–7.5 hours per week. The reduction in mortality continues to increase with the amount of exercise, but then the benefits start to level off. For individuals who exercise more than 75 hours per week, the reduction in mortality actually declines to the same level as those who exercise between 7.5 and 15 hours a week. (Another reason not to work out 12 hours a day.)

Now, let's chart the data:

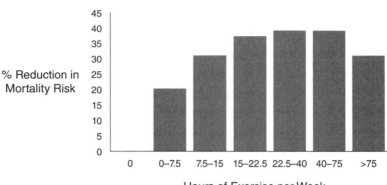

FIGURE 6-3

This chart shows the increased benefits of exercising, and how that increase actually tapers off (and then declines) with more exercise.

Now, let's see how we can manipulate the data.

Pretend you own a gym, and you want to show your casual customers how much longer they might live if they would just exercise more often. So you take the data and make a chart like this:

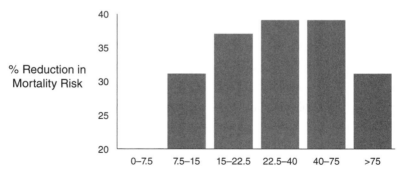

FIGURE 6-4

This chart uses the *exact same data* as the first chart. All we did was eliminate the data for 0 hours (we've done this for all subsequent charts), start the y-axis (the vertical axis) at 20 (instead of 0) and cut it off at 40, which is just above our most extreme data point. See the difference? And—perhaps more importantly—do you see how this chart would make you want to head to the gym more than 7.5 hours a week?

If we really wanted to emphasize the benefits of exercise, we could cut off the x-axis (the horizontal axis) at the 22.5 to 40 hours increment as shown here, and eliminate the plateau and decline:

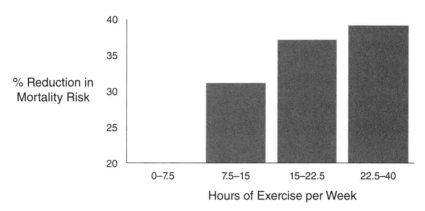

FIGURE 6-5

With this chart, we've made it appear as if exercising leads to only increasing benefits.

Now, imagine your spouse has been bugging you to hit the gym to be healthier and live longer. You're happy being a couch potato, so you want to *minimize* the benefits of exercising. So you take the data and make a chart like this:

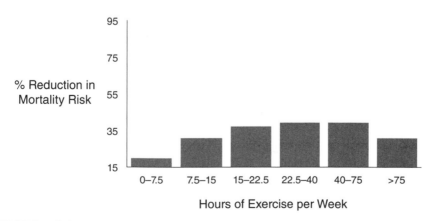

FIGURE 6-6

Again, it's the *same exact data*. In this case, we simply started the y-axis at 15 and ended it at 95, which has the effect of not only minimizing the height of each bar, but also minimizing the perceived differences (risk reductions) between them.

Of course, if we really wanted to confuse you—or try to make you think you shouldn't exercise—we could create a chart like this:

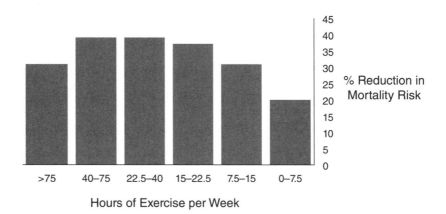

FIGURE 6-7

See what we did there? In bar charts, you usually see the x-axis increasing from left to right. By flipping the x-axis, we can make it appear as if the benefit increases slightly but then *decreases*, unless you really take the time to read and understand all of the labels.

These types of tactics are something to watch for in all types of data representations. For example, a pie chart is commonly used to show the various percentages of different groups within a full data set, all of which typically add up to 100 percent. So imagine our surprise when we saw a pie chart in which the total added up to 193 percent.[11]

Just as the x-axis typically increases left to right, the y-axis usually increases from bottom to top. But if we flip the y-axis, now the bars go down instead of up, implying (at first glance) a negative relationship. Here's what that looks like:

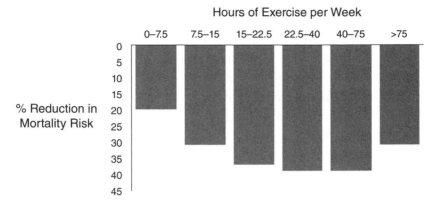

FIGURE 6-8

Another thing to look for in charts is whether the data is *cumulative* or *incremental*. For example, what if we looked at this data in terms of *incremental* gains? How much *additional* benefit can we enjoy with each increment of exercise? That chart would look like this:

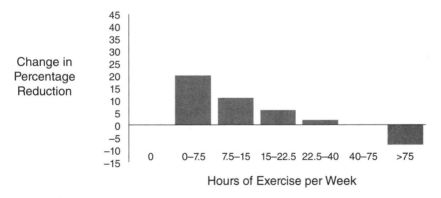

FIGURE 6-9

Big difference, right? You can see that you get the biggest bang for your buck just by showing up for a few hours each week, and then it's diminishing returns after that—to the point of actually causing harm after 75 hours.

On the other hand, showing cumulative rather than incremental data is a common tactic in business, because it can turn a negative story into a positive one. In one real-world example, a well-known technology company highlighted smartphone sales by showing cumulative sales of its phones. As expected, the bars keep going up and up from left to right, since—with a cumulative chart—each quarter's sales are simply added to all of the sales that came before. What the chart didn't show is that sales had actually declined in previous quarters. But as long as the company sells at least some phones each quarter, a decrease doesn't look like a decrease on a cumulative graph—it just looks like less of an increase.[12]

If you have 10 minutes and you know how to use a spreadsheet application, you can come up with a dozen different ways to display the same exact data. And the way that data is displayed makes a *huge* difference in terms of the story it suggests to the reader. As a sound consumer of data, you can think about how the underlying data is being graphed and what it might be really telling you.[13]

ROUND AND ROUND

In a bar chart, you're usually just comparing the height of bars (or width, for horizontal charts). But if you have a visual that uses circles, things can get a bit tricky.

Taking data from the Bureau of Labor Statistics, we can actually break down how the average American spends the day, hour by hour.[14] Let's take a look at how much time we spend watching TV versus socializing—unsurprisingly, it's heavily skewed in favor of TV. In 2014, we spent an average of 2.82 hours per day watching TV and .71 hours per day socializing.

So, you draw two circles, with the area of each circle representing the amount of time. You get a comparison that looks like this:

Socializing

Watching TV

FIGURE 6-10

Okay, so we spend more time watching TV, but not *that* much more, right?

Now, let's do the same thing, with the same data—except let's use the *diameter* of each circle to represent the amount of time. Your new chart looks like this:

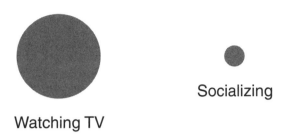

Watching TV   Socializing

FIGURE 6-11

Ouch. Based on this chart, it looks like we're spending *way* too much time in front of the boob tube.

Why? Because math. Simply put, a circle's diameter and area are not the same thing. As any middle school kid can tell you, the area of a circle equals pi times the radius squared ($A=\pi r^2$). So, when you *double* a circle's diameter, you actually *quadruple* the circle's area.

As you can see from this example, using the diameter of a circle to represent data gives you different results than using the area of a circle. Statistically speaking, neither method is wrong, per se. Some people would argue that using the area to represent data makes more sense, since using the diameter often confuses people. After all, if you're just going to use diameter (a straight line), why not simply show a bar chart?

Countless hours (and legal fees) have been spent debating these exact issues. Our goal isn't to provide a definitive answer, but simply to make you stop and ask some questions the next time you see data represented in circles.[15]

WORTH 1,000 WORDS

Visuals can also be used to make data seem more trustworthy. As the *Harvard Business Review* noted, citing research from Cornell, "When a claim about a new drug's effectiveness was presented in text form, 67%

of research participants said they believed it. But when the text was accompanied by a simple graph making exactly the same claim, 97% believed it."[16] This reflects a bias we see in some cases, in which an effect isn't measured statistically, but rather just asserted visually or otherwise. (This is similar to "Ipse dixit" bias. Ipse dixit is Latin for "he himself said it," and it's used when an expert says something is true because, well, she said so. Just like when you would ask your parents why you had to go to bed, and their answer was "because we said so." In fact, next time your kids ask why they have to do something, we highly recommend responding simply with "ipse dixit.")

The next time you're watching TV, take note of how many commercials feature someone in a lab coat, which is typically a visual sign of medical or scientific expertise. The implication is clear—this is someone you should trust.

We agree that good experts are often more knowledgeable and trustworthy than the average person, and can use their knowledge to help broaden our understanding of important issues. But simply putting on a lab coat (or scrubs, or even a suit) doesn't make someone an expert.

Remember, every time you see an image, it's because someone decided it should be there, often to serve a specific purpose. On restaurant menus, for example, icons and photos have been shown to increase sales up to 30 percent.[17]

But perhaps we need to look at visuals more closely. As a data journalist explained in a fascinating piece for the *Guardian*, "diagrams and data visualisations are overwhelmingly used simply as a medium of displaying final results. The result is that reading text and thinking 'I disagree with this' comes much more naturally to us than looking at a well-presented map or line graph and thinking the same."[18]

We've said it before and we'll say it again: your goal as an educated consumer of data should be to keep digging until you get to the real information. It's not always easy to do. Why? As noted ad man and author Bob Hoffman said in an e-mail exchange, "Most of the reported studies that we see in business do not give us the primary data or access to the questionnaire or methodology. Instead they give us a chart or two and some conclusions. Consequently, it's very difficult to know if the study was conducted in a proper manner."

TESTING ONE, TWO, THREE

Another way in which data is misrepresented is by treating all data equally, even when it's not.

Let's say you have a friend who's opposed to animal testing, and he sends you a list of companies that test their products on animals, asking you to boycott these businesses.[19]

If you just see a list of these companies, or a page filled with their logos, then the implication is that each of these companies bears equal responsibility for testing on animals. But is that really the case?

Do all of these companies do the same amount of testing on animals? Do they all use the same types of chemicals? Do they all test on the same types of animals?

In reality, it's unlikely that these companies are all equal in the ways that they test their products on animals, yet they're all treated equally when they're simply listed on a page. It's like texting your wife that you ate "french fries and carrots" for a snack. Was it 10 of each? Or 2 carrots and 50 french fries? When all data is treated equally, that can be a form of misrepresentation.

The TV talk show host John Oliver illustrated this concept brilliantly when he hosted a debate about climate change.[20] Instead of typical TV debates that feature one or two people on each side of an issue, Oliver decided to have a representative number of people on each side. So he invited 97 people to argue that climate change is real—and 3 to argue that it's not. With that one simple action, he completely changed the way the average person perceives the debate—which, we presume, was exactly his point.

THE ONE AND ONLY

Consider the following sentences:

Twenty-two percent of shark attacks are fatal.
Only 22 percent of shark attacks are fatal.

By adding the word "only," we minimized the data that follows—another way to misrepresent data. As a statistician for the Bureau of Labor Statistics explained, "the word 'only' evokes an unrealistic expectation of something different."[21]

Adding or omitting words is a common way of misrepresenting data.

In his *Ad Contrarian* blog, Bob Hoffman wrote about an oft-repeated statistic that 60 percent of people say they use QR (quick response) codes.[22] "This statistic was obviously total bullshit," noted Hoffman, "and yet serious people seemed to be taking it seriously. Anyone who spent any time in the real world could see that *no one* was using QR codes."[23]

So where did the 60 percent come from? Perhaps, as Hoffman theorizes, this was the percentage of people who have *ever* used a QR code. In framing the data without context, Hoffman notes that, "a truth is technically being told, but reality is being radically misrepresented."

Here's the lesson—if you take data at face value, you may not be getting the full story. You don't know if the data is being misrepresented—or omitted—unless you ask.

MILES TO GO

Sometimes, data is purposefully misrepresented to help you rather than mislead you.

If you've ever driven a car that's low on gas, you may have noticed something surprising—even when the needle on the gas gauge shows that the tank is empty, you can usually keep driving. According to the data (the fuel gauge), you shouldn't have any gas left. And yet, you do.

Assuming your gauge isn't broken, there's a good reason for this—auto manufacturers know that most people don't like to run out of gas. According to an ABC News report, Ford, GM, and Chrysler all provide a "buffer" for American drivers (although not always for drivers in other countries, who may have more exacting expectations).[24]

So what do some manufacturers do? Present the data in a way that makes it *appear* as if you have less fuel than you really do. So the next time your gas gauge hits E—and you haven't run out of gas—make sure you thank whoever made your car.

FAKES AND MISTAKES

Did you hear about the 17,000 British men who got pregnant?

In a letter to the *British Medical Journal*, three physicians cited statistics showing that more than 17,000 men received inpatient obstetric services through England's NHS (National Health Service).[25]

Of course, it's not true. You can barely get some guys to change a diaper, let alone carry a baby inside them for nine months. The men were most likely "pregnant" due to a medical coding error. In other words, someone typed in the wrong data during a doctor's visit.

Here are a few more classic examples:

■ *Something's fishy*—Fifty-nine percent of tuna samples purchased from a store or restaurant were mislabeled; oftentimes, the fish was actually escolar, a snake mackerel that can cause something referred to in polite company as gastrointestinal distress.[26]

■ *Aim for the (fake) stars*—In an undercover operation, the New York State Office of the Attorney General found companies writing fake online reviews for businesses on Yelp, Google Local, and other websites—a practice known as "astroturfing."

■ *Fat-free isn't*—The U.S. Food and Drug Administration (FDA) allows foods with less than half a gram of fat per serving to still be called "fat-free." So, if you eat more than one serving of a few "fat-free" foods per day, you could easily be consuming a few grams of fat.[27]

■ *Tough cell*—It was, as *Bloomberg Business* called it, "the Excel Error that Changed History."[28] Two Harvard University economists—Carmen Reinhart and Kenneth Rogoff—ended up in the headlines for all the wrong reasons when they made a spreadsheet mistake in a paper that examined the effects of government debt on economic growth.

They forgot to include five rows in one of their calculations, which made a key result turn out to be -0.1 percent instead of +0.2 percent. (Economists have pointed out other errors that would make the calculation even further off base.)

DOT YOUR I'S, CROSS YOUR T'S, AND WATCH THE S&P

Then there was the time false data wiped out $136 billion in value from the stock market.

On April 23, 2013, the following message was sent from the Associated Press Twitter account:

"Breaking: Two Explosions in the White House and Barack Obama is injured."

Investors panicked, stock prices plummeted, and the S&P 500 lost more than $136 billion over the course of just two minutes.

All because of a hoax.

The markets recovered quickly, as people realized the tweet wasn't true. There were no explosions. President Obama wasn't injured. But

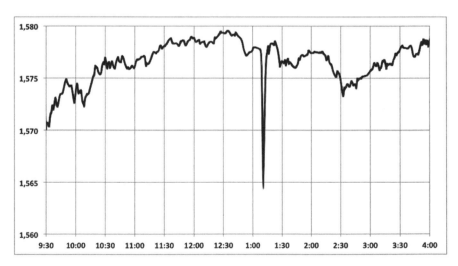

FIGURE 6-12   You can see the dramatic dip in the S&P 500 index just after 1 p.m.

if you owned stocks or mutual funds, for a few tense minutes that fake data had some very real repercussions for your portfolio.

WHERE DOES DATA COME FROM?

To finish up on misrepresentation, let's talk about good old *Wikipedia*. Many a college term paper has been written with help from the site, which offers, in its own words, "openly editable content."[29]

It's that last part—"openly editable"—that should give you pause as a smart consumer of data. When virtually anyone with an Internet connection can update one of the world's most popular websites, how can you trust the results? The short answer is that you can't.[30] As the site notes, "while some articles are of the highest quality of scholarship, others are admittedly complete rubbish."[31]

So, if you are going to rely on *Wikipedia*, make sure you check the underlying sources.

"EXPIRATION" DATES

So far in this chapter, we've focused on examples of data being *misrepresented*—a person, company, or organization is giving you data that isn't quite true.

On the flip side, you need to make sure you're not *misinterpreting* data that *is* true.

For example, if you're one of those people who throws out food as soon as it passes the date stamped on the package, you're probably wasting hundreds of dollars or more each year. That's because what most of us interpret as food expiration dates really aren't expiration dates at all.

According to the Food Safety and Inspection Service at the U.S. Department of Agriculture (USDA), it turns out that many foods are fine for consumption after the dates on the product. In fact, the dates represent not expiration, but in most cases, the dates at which the product would be at its peak quality. (Some states require dating for some foods, but in general federal regulations don't require dating of foods, except for infant formula.)

Here are the guidelines, straight from the USDA's website:[32]

- A **"Sell-By"** date tells the store how long to display the product for sale. You should buy the product before the date expires.
- A **"Best if Used By (or Before)"** date is recommended for best flavor or quality. It is not a purchase or safety date.
- A **"Use-By"** date is the last date recommended for the use of the product while at peak quality. The date has been determined by the manufacturer of the product. (That said, the USDA often recommends consuming food by the "use-by" date. It also recommends keeping your eggs in the coldest part of your refrigerator—not in the door.)

With three different types of dates—none of which are truly expiration dates—it's easy to be confused about what the underlying data means. In fact, confusion over dates "leads nine out of 10 Americans to needlessly throw away food,"[33] according to the Natural Resources Defense Council (NRDC), citing a study from the Food Marketing Institute.

So-called "expiration dates" are an excellent lesson in everydata, because they illustrate the importance of knowing what the data stands for. Food manufacturers aren't misrepresenting the "expiration date" data. But the way in which you interpret this data could be taking a big bite out of your budget.[34]

NEST EGG (ON THEIR FACE)

When Google announced that it was buying Nest—the thermostat company—some people thought they could make a few dollars by buying stock in the company that trades as NEST. In just one day (January 14, 2014), NEST stock went up 1900 percent.

Unfortunately for the get-rich-quick crowd, NEST is *not* the ticker name for Nest—it's the name for Nestor, a company that sells traffic enforcement systems. (Nest, the thermostat company, was not a publicly traded company, although as of 2015 it is owned by Alphabet, the holding company created by Google.) Nestor had gone into receivership in 2009, and had no assets.

The data was accurate. The news about Google buying Nest was true. But investors didn't check their facts and ended up buying a penny stock instead of the latest Google acquisition. (Nestor's share price did drop—although not as quickly as it rose. Even at the close of day on January 14, 2014, it was trading approximately 400 percent higher than it was when the market opened that day.)

IGNORANCE IS NOT BLISS

Americans are bad at math. Like, really bad. In one study, the U.S. ranked 21st out of 23 countries.[35] Perhaps that explains why A&W Restaurants' burger was a flop.

As reported by the *New York Times Magazine*, back in the early 1980s, the A&W restaurant chain wanted to compete with McDonald's and its famous Quarter Pounder.[36] So A&W decided to come out with the Third Pounder. Customers thought it tasted better, but it just wasn't selling. Apparently people thought a quarter pound (1/4) was bigger than a third of a pound (1/3).

Why would they think 1/4 is bigger than 1/3? Because 4 is bigger than 3.

Yes, seriously.

People misinterpreted the size of a burger because they couldn't understand fractions.

In our work, we've found that many people have a hard time comparing numbers, fractions, and percentages. One famous study found that people "rated cancer as riskier when it was described as 'kills 1,286 out of 10,000 people' than as 'kills 24.14 out of 100 people.'"[37] (The statistics are based on a previous study, in which naïve participants were asked to estimate death rates.)

If you do the math, it's easy to see that 1,286 out of 10,000 people is a smaller percentage than 24.14 out of 100. The problem is that a lot of people don't know how to do the math—or they simply assume that the first option must be riskier because 1,286 is more than 24.14.

How do you fix this problem? Other than going back in time and becoming a third-grade math teacher, consider putting all data in the same format if you want people to compare it.

We understand that it's not easy (for many people) to see that 24.14/100 is bigger than 1,286/10,000. But it's hard to argue with the fact that 2,414 is more than 1,286.

How to Be a Smart Consumer of Data That Is Misrepresented (or Could Be Misinterpreted)

There are countless ways in which data can be misrepresented or misinterpreted, but here are five things you can do as a smart consumer of data, starting right now:

1. For charts and graphs, **take a close look at the x-axis and y-axis**. It's easy for someone to tell a very different story with the data simply by adjusting the scale, height, or other aspects of one (or both) of the axes. Where does the scale start and end? Are the numbers going up or down? Does the chart or graph include all of the relevant data? These are a few of the questions you can ask.

2. **Pay attention to the language**. What exactly do the words say? If a factory says it hasn't had any accidents "recently," what does that mean? And who defines what an "accident" is? You don't have to cross-examine everyone you meet, but understand that what people don't say can often be as important as what they do say.

3. **Verify your source**. Just because you see it on the Internet (or hear it from your boss, or read it in the newspaper, or watch it on TV...) doesn't mean it's true. The earth is round. But you might think otherwise if you believe the Flat Earth Society.[38]

4. **Make sure it's not a mistake**. As the *Telegraph* noted, "almost one in five large businesses have suffered financial losses as a result of errors in spreadsheets," citing a report from consulting firm F1F9.[39] Double-check your work. Then check it again.

5. **Interpret the data correctly**. Are you buying the stock you think you're buying? Do you know what the expiration date on the carton of eggs really means? Are you confused about the difference between fractions, decimals, and percentages? Sometimes the data is correct—but it's misinterpreted due to haste, ignorance, or other factors.

7

Spoonfed Data

When Cherry Picking Goes Bananas

Imagine it's 1996 and you're the parent of a bouncing baby girl. You just put her to bed, and you're sitting down to watch TV for a few well-deserved minutes.

A commercial comes on, showing jars of baby food along with pictures of fresh apples and carrots. You want the best for your baby, so you pay attention to what the ad is saying, even as you're wiping baby drool off your favorite sweater.[1]

You see a smiling baby. You see the jars of baby food. You hear the announcer tell you how great this baby food is, and then you hear the voice say, "To learn more why four out of five pediatricians who recommend baby food recommend Gerber, call us anytime, day or night."[2]

Gerber repeated the claim in a phone recording for consumers. When people called the number, they heard an announcer say, "four out of five pediatricians who recommend baby food recommend Gerber."

Four out of five pediatricians. Sounds like a pretty solid endorsement, doesn't it?

Especially if you're a sleep-deprived parent. And if four out of five pediatricians recommend Gerber, that means only one single pediatrician didn't, right? Not quite.

The fact is that only about 12 percent of all the pediatricians the company surveyed actually recommended Gerber. So how did it get to "four out of five"?

The problem was that Gerber *cherry-picked* the data. You've probably heard of cherry-picking. In fact, you've probably done it yourself. Cherry-picking just means that you're picking anecdotal examples from the data to make your point, while ignoring other data points that may contradict it. Gerber certainly isn't the only firm to have ever cherry-picked data to sell its product. But in this particular example, the Federal Trade Commission (FTC)—a U.S. government agency whose mission includes preventing deceptive and unfair business practices—investigated the nature of Gerber's claims, which they called "false and misleading."[3]

Gerber wasn't saying that four out of five pediatricians recommended its baby food. The company was saying that *of the pediatricians who recommended baby food*, four out of five recommended Gerber. The company cherry-picked the results from a *purposely* selected sample of the data, by only taking answers from pediatricians who recommended baby food.

It's an important distinction, especially because, at the time, many pediatricians didn't recommend baby food at all due to concerns about added sugar, fillers, and other ingredients. In this case, more than a quarter of the pediatricians Gerber surveyed didn't recommend baby food at all.[4] If Gerber had included these pediatricians in its results, it couldn't have made the four out of five claim.

To Gerber's credit, it was actually up front about how it used this sample of pediatricians and cherry-picked the data. In every case that we saw, Gerber qualified its claims by telling consumers that it was only talking about pediatricians who recommended baby food.

But Gerber also cherry-picked the data in another, less obvious way.

Gerber started by surveying 562 pediatricians, to be exact. And of those, according to the FTC, "408 responded that they recommend baby food to their patients at least once per week."[5] Based on the claim "four out of five pediatricians who recommend baby food recommend Gerber," you would expect that most of these 408 pediatricians endorsed Gerber.

Not quite. See, Gerber didn't just cherry-pick the data. It cherry-picked data that had already been cherry-picked.

Because out of the 408 pediatricians who recommended baby food, *332 of them didn't recommend a specific brand.* They just said their patients should eat baby food at least once a week.

In other words, Gerber didn't count the pediatricians who didn't

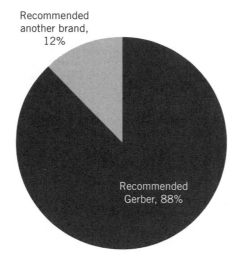

FIGURE 7-1   Pediatricians who recommended a specific brand of baby food.

recommend a specific brand of baby food. All they included in their results were the pediatricians who (A) recommended baby food and (B) recommended a specific brand.

Yes, four out of five of those cherry-picked pediatricians recommended Gerber. But—if you look at all the data—that only represented 12 percent of the full data set, and still only 16 percent of the cherry-picked sample (pediatricians who recommended baby food).

Here are the numbers:

- Gerber started with 562 pediatricians.
- 408 responded that they recommend baby food.
- 76 recommended a specific brand.
- 67 recommended Gerber.

So, if you were a parent who saw or heard one of these ads, you might think that four out of five pediatricians recommended Gerber. Even if you paid attention and noticed the cherry-picked data, you might think that four out of five pediatricians *who recommended baby food* recommended Gerber. Either way, you would be wrong.

The director of the Federal Trade Commission's Bureau of Consumer Protection at the time (Jodie Bernstein) said it best: "Consumers

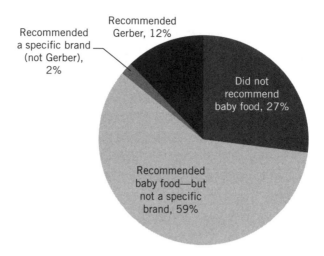

FIGURE 7-2   All pediatricians surveyed.

were led to believe that Gerber had competent or reliable studies proving that four out of five doctors recommend Gerber. But Gerber skewed the results of the study by weeding out doctors who don't recommend baby food at all and those who don't recommend specific brands."[6]

The Federal Trade Commission (FTC)—prompted by a petition from the Center for Science in the Public Interest—filed a complaint against Gerber. Even though Gerber had clearly stated that it was only talking about pediatricians who recommended baby food, the FTC said that Gerber "represented, expressly or by implication, that approximately four out of five pediatricians recommend Gerber."

In other words, even though Gerber *told* people it was cherry-picking the data by only including pediatricians who recommended baby food, the FTC still felt that some consumers might think the statistic applied to all pediatricians. The FTC didn't think that consumers could properly interpret cherry-picked data, even when it was right there in black and white.

The FTC also faulted Gerber for apparently failing to disclose the fact that it was only counting pediatricians who recommended a specific brand of baby food.

In a consent order—which, we should note, is for settlement purposes only, and not an admission that the law has been violated, or even an admission that the alleged facts (other than jurisdictional ones) are true—Gerber agreed that any future "recommendation, approval, or endorsement" of a product by professionals had to rely upon "competent and reliable scientific evidence, that substantiates the representation."[7]

WHAT IS CHERRY PICKING?

The phrase "cherry picking" likely comes from the physical act of hand-picking cherries from a tree.[8] Think about it—if you're out in the cherry orchard with your bucket and ladder, your job is to fill the bucket with cherries that you can sell at the market. So you're going to skip any cherries that look bruised or aren't ripe yet, and you're going to fill your bucket with the best-looking cherries you can pick. Hence, cherry picking—when you're selecting only the data (cherries) that other people want.

There are, of course, other meanings for "cherry picking," like choosing to only pick the lowest-hanging fruit (metaphorically speaking). For example, in basketball, a "cherry picker" is a player who hangs out near the other team's basket waiting for a long pass from a teammate so he or she can make an easy layup or dunk. (In water polo, the same tactic is called "sea gulling," possibly because seagulls look for easy ways to score food.)

But, for our purposes, we're going to talk about cherry picking in terms of choosing the most favorable data—and ignoring other data that runs counter to the desired result—in order to make a point. Or, as one study put it, "taking the best and leaving the rest."[9]

So why do you need to watch out for cherry picking? As we saw in chapter 2, when you look at different samples of the same data, you can get very different results. When you do it deliberately, you can try to do it in a way that gives you the results you want.

Consider a small restaurant that's open from lunch through dinnertime. One day, every hour on the hour, the restaurateurs count how many people are in the restaurant. Here's what they find:

11 a.m. – 2 people
12 p.m. – 25 people
1 p.m. – 30 people

2 p.m. – 3 people
3 p.m. – 0 people
4 p.m. – 2 people
5 p.m. – 28 people
6 p.m. – 35 people
7 p.m. – 5 people
8 p.m. – 3 people

The next day, a potential buyer comes in and wants to know how business is doing. "Great," the owners say. "We were packed for lunch and dinner—people were lined up out the door!" The potential buyer leaves, ready to put in a nice big offer for the small restaurant.

Two minutes later, in walks the restaurant's landlord, who tells the restaurateurs that she wants to double their rent. "You can't do that!" say the owners. "This place is practically empty most of the time!"

Of course, both statements are 100 percent true—and 100 percent cherry picked. If you only look at the data for the lunch and dinner rush, the restaurant is full. If you only look at the times in between lunch and dinner, the restaurant is nearly empty. Same data—different cherry-picked samples—and wildly different results.

THINGS HAPPEN IN THREES... AND FOURS... AND FIVES...

Many of the patterns we think we see in our daily lives aren't patterns at all, but rather the result of good old-fashioned cherry picking.

Think about the notion that good things happen in threes. Or bad things happen in threes. Or maybe it's bad things happen to good people in threes. Is it true? Or are you just cherry-picking the data?

In June of 2009, Michael Jackson, Farrah Fawcett, and Ed McMahon all died within the same week. Just another example that celebrity deaths happen in threes, right?

But what about Billy Mays, who died a few days later? Or Walter Cronkite, who died in July of 2009? Or John Updike, who died the previous January?

"The death-in-threes claim is empty and uselessly flexible in at least two senses," wrote a math professor in a commentary posted by ABC News.[10] "Not only is the time frame unspecified, but so is the definition of celebrity."

In other words, if you want to claim that the deaths of Jackson, Fawcett, and McMahon proved that celebrity deaths happen in threes, you have to (A) limit your sample set to June 23 to June 25, 2009, and (B) decide who is, and who isn't, a celebrity. Are we only talking about celebrities in California, or throughout the United States? Why not throughout the world? When we looked at it, the *Wikipedia* page for 2009 deaths didn't list Ed McMahon (lesson: don't be the side-kick), but it did include a Japanese professional wrestler and a German–British social theorist and politician, both of whom also died in June of 2009.[11]

So, if you want to find an example of three celebrities who died around the same time, you can. And if you want to find an example of two celebrities who died around the same time, you can do that too. Or four celebrities. Or five. Or whatever you want. *It all depends on how you define celebrity, and what time frame you're looking at.* In other words, it all depends on how you sample—and cherry-pick—the data.

Remember this: if you're in a situation where you can select whatever data you want to support your position, you may be cherry-picking.

AMERICA'S PASTIME

If you're a sports fan, you've probably seen and heard more than your fair share of cherry-picked statistics. Imagine this: it's 1988, and you're watching game one of the World Series. It's the Oakland A's versus the LA Dodgers. Bottom of the ninth, two outs. We're just a few minutes away from watching Kirk Gibson hit one of the most memorable home runs in baseball history, when this statistic appears on your TV screen: "In the last 10 years, the team that lost game one has gone on to win 7 of the 10 series."[12]

How is this cherry-picking? First of all, the broadcasters only chose to talk about teams that won or lost game one of the World Series. We suppose that's understandable given that that's the game being broadcast. But why would they limit the sample set to the past 10 years? Why not 5? Or 20? Or 30? Will the data still tell the same story with a different sample set?[13]

Take a look—or listen—for these types of cherry-picked statistics the next time you're watching a game, listening to one on the radio, or reading the sports section of the newspaper. Are these types of stats entertaining? Absolutely. Do they help pass the time in between pitches, snaps, and passes? Of course. But are they useful? Not really. Many times, they're shakier than Kirk Gibson's legs were on that historic day back in 1988.

Okay, so we understand that cherry-picking statistics during a baseball game doesn't really have much of an impact on anything. But what about cherry-picking statistics that can cost you $100,000?

HOME SWEET HOME

Buying a house is typically the biggest investment you'll make. Which is why you don't want to rely on cherry-picked data when making your decision.

Let's say it's 2012, you and your spouse are tired of living in a small apartment, and decide you want to buy a house. You mention it during Sunday dinner at your in-laws' house, at which point your father-in-law puts down his forkful of turkey and says it's the worst investment you could make, since housing prices are down nearly 20 percent. That's not true, you counter respectfully (because who wants to start a fight with her father-in-law?). You point out that home prices have actually *increased* approximately 180 percent.

So who's right? You both are—which is good, because nobody wants to sleep on the couch.

Here's a graph of housing prices that your father-in-law relies on for his claim that housing prices have plummeted over the last five years. It seems pretty indisputable, no?

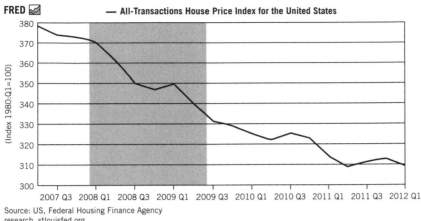

FIGURE 7-3 U.S. Federal Housing Finance Agency, All-Transactions House Price Index for the United States (USSTHPI), retrieved from FRED, Federal Reserve Bank of St. Louis, August 25, 2015. (https://research.stlouisfed.org/fred2/series/USSTHPI/)

But your father-in-law was only looking at the past five years of data. Here is the graph *you* had in mind for housing prices, taking the long-run view over the past decades.

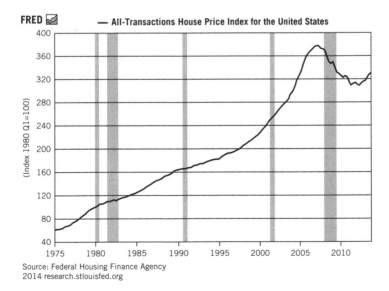

FIGURE 7-4 U.S. Federal Housing Finance Agency, All-Transactions House Price Index for the United States (USSTHPI), retrieved from FRED, Federal Reserve Bank of St. Louis, August 25, 2015. (https://research.stlouisfed.org/fred2/series/USSTHPI/)

Sure, there was a slight dip in prices. But when you take the long view, you can see that house prices have actually increased over 180 percent since 1982.

An argument over the dinner table may be informative, and perhaps you feel justified to have trumped your father-in-law after all. But what about even higher-stakes arguments—like the debate over global warming?

The *Skeptical Science* website published charts showing how you could use the same exact data to show that the earth's surface is warming—or to show that it isn't—depending on how you view the data.[14] For example, if you look at the data over a period of approximately 45 years, it's clear that there is an upward trend in the temperature change.

However, if you take the *same exact data* but only look at shorter periods of time, perhaps only 8 or 10 years at a time, then you can easily make charts that show a slight downward trend in temperature.

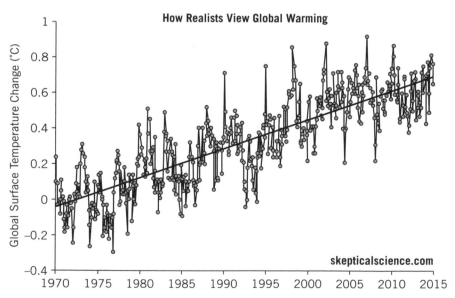

FIGURE 7-5   Created by Dana Nuccitelli for Skeptical Science. (SkepticalScience .com)

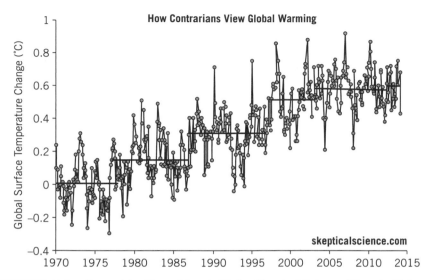

FIGURE 7-6 Created by Dana Nuccitelli for *Skeptical Science*. (SkepticalScience .com)

Same data. Completely contradictory results. All because of cherry-picking.

CAST YOUR VOTE

So, we've talked about one of the most trusted groups of people (pediatricians). Now, let's talk about one of the least trusted groups.

Politicians know all about cherry-picking. If you're running for office and you're speaking at an NRA fundraiser, you're going to highlight your experience growing up hunting with your dad in the backwoods of Kentucky. But if you're hosting a fundraiser in Hollywood, you're going to talk about your famous actor uncle on your mom's side of the family.

And when it comes to your opponents, cherry picking is as common as an American flag lapel pin. The political landscape is littered with men and women whose candidacies fell apart after their opponents cherry-picked negative quotes, votes, and photographs.

Here's an example. During the 1988 presidential campaign, Vice President George H. W. Bush implied Massachusetts governor Michael Dukakis was soft on crime, given that Dukakis had allowed for a weekend furlough for Willie Horton, who went on to commit both rape and murder. A television commercial took full advantage of this fact, stating that "Michael Dukakis not only opposes the death penalty, he allowed first-degree murderers to have weekend passes from prison."[15] The TV spot was a turning point in the race, and helped Vice President Bush defeat Dukakis.

Perhaps the race would have turned out differently if viewers knew that "99.5 percent of the 11,000 furloughed inmates have returned to prison on schedule," as one reporter pointed out.[16] Willie Horton was apparently part of the other .5 percent.

Another type of cherry picking is called quote mining. Here's an example: On November 28, 2003, Condoleezza Rice—then serving as President George W. Bush's national security advisor—appeared on CBS's *Early Show*.

If you watch the movie *Fahrenheit 9/11*, you'll hear a quote from Ms. Rice's appearance. "Oh, indeed there is a tie between Iraq and what happened on 9/11," she says, before the camera cuts away.[17]

Here's the full quote: "Oh, indeed there is a tie between Iraq and what happened on 9/11. It's not that Saddam Hussein was somehow himself and his regime involved in 9/11, but, if you think about what caused 9/11, it is the rise of ideologies of hatred that lead people to drive airplanes into buildings in New York."[18] Quite a different statement from the one made in just the first sentence.

Rice's particular quote in the movie appears to be taken out of context and cherry-picked. *Fahrenheit 9/11* was made by filmmaker and activist Michael Moore, who admitted that his goal was to change people's minds and influence the upcoming presidential election.[19] Should we *expect* that someone with an agenda is going to cherry-pick? How do we know what the person's agenda is when we're walking into a movie theater, picking up a book, or just having a conversation with someone?

In many cases we can't—which is why it's important to keep asking questions to uncover as much data as possible if you want to know the real story.

TRUST US—WE'RE IN ADVERTISING

So why do products and brands cherry-pick data? Because it lets them stand out. And standing out is key. When we checked the Colgate website, for example, we found 31 types of Colgate toothpaste.[20] That seems like a lot, considering you only have 32 teeth. We went to a local grocery store to check out the toothpaste aisle, and found more than a dozen types of Colgate—not to mention Crest, Aim, Arm & Hammer, Tom's of Maine (which is owned by Colgate-Palmolive), and others. Brands are competing against other companies—and against themselves.

As we saw with Gerber, advertising is an excellent source for finding cherry-picked data. Why? Because it works. And because it's how advertisers are taught to sell products.

When you watch a TV commercial, oftentimes everything you see and hear has been cherry picked. Everything. The actors are carefully chosen based on their age, gender, ethnicity, weight, hairstyle, number of freckles, and so on. Typically, every word in the script has been scrutinized by at least a dozen people. Watch closely, and you'll probably see a piece of clothing or prop that has been picked because it is the same color as the brand's logo. Few things in a TV commercial are there by accident—which is why it can easily take a 12-hour day just to film a 30-second commercial, not to mention the days (or weeks) it takes for editing.

But before you start criticizing advertisers for spending all this time (and money) to sell you a new pair of shoes or breakfast cereal or life insurance, take a look in the mirror.

Seriously, take a look in the mirror. Every time you get dressed up for a date or job interview, you're cherry-picking items from your closet to make you look your best. Does that mean you should say, "Wow, great cherry-picking!" when your date shows up at your door? Probably not—at least not if you want a second date. But it's just another example of how we all cherry-pick, every single day.[21]

YOU'RE A CHERRY PICKER—YES, YOU

By now, you should be able to think of at least a few ways that you have cherry-picked data throughout your life. For example, you may have:

- Filled out an online dating profile
- Written a recommendation letter for a coworker
- Neglected to tell your spouse about that weekend in Vegas
- Decided not to mow the lawn because it might rain

In all of these cases, you didn't use all of the data you had. You only used the data you wanted to use.

Often, it's literally impossible to include all the data. Think about your résumé or LinkedIn profile. These are, by definition, summaries of what you have done, and (in most cases) are designed to help you get a better job. So of course you're going to only list the highlights of your career and only include those that paint you in a positive light. But it's still cherry picking. You know it. Your boss knows it. And the human resources manager definitely knows it. Which is why interviews are often designed to uncover the data that is not listed on your résumé.

SEEING THE FOREST FOR THE (CHERRY) TREES

As you can see, there are many different ways to cherry-pick data. You can choose to "take the best and leave the rest" when it comes to:

- Dates or times (home prices over a 5-year versus 10-year period)
- Groups or subgroups (four out of five pediatricians *who recommend baby food* recommend Gerber)
- Past results ("In World Series history, 15 teams won Game 1 by at least six runs, yet only 8 of those went on to a championship."[22])
- Vague or arbitrary labels (who do you categorize as a "celebrity" when you say that celebrity deaths happen in threes?)

- Factors that aren't made public but could be selected in a nonrandom way (search engine results with Google, Bing, etc.)
- People (surveying only predominantly right- or left-leaning individuals in a state about their voting preferences is likely to provide different results than surveying 1,000 people at random per state—we looked at sampling in chapter 2)

But, in order to know if the data has been cherry picked, you have to know how much original data exists—which goes back to the sampling issues we talked about in chapter 2. If you're studying climate change, do you have temperature readings from every continent, taken every second over the past 1,000 years? Of course not. In many cases, there's a good chance you don't have *all* the data. Perhaps nobody does—or maybe somebody does and you're only seeing some of it.

As you think about cherry picking, watch out for outlier data—unique data points that don't really advance our understanding of the relationship we are studying. You probably know someone who claims he can "beat the market" by cherry-picking individual stocks, or funds, or industries. But these people could be considered outliers; even professional mutual fund managers consistently perform below the market.[23]

Cherry picking isn't the only data tactic that can skew the results by ignoring all of the data. You also need to watch out for:

- *Claims based on anecdotal evidence*—If you are only relying on anecdotes (that is, select stories about something), then you do not have all of the data. For example, if you hear that your neighbor got sick after eating at a restaurant, you can't assume that everyone who eats at that restaurant is also going to get sick.[24]

- *Attentional bias*—This happens when you pay more attention to some data than to other data. The difference between attentional bias and cherry picking is that with cherry picking you are specifically choosing which data to include and which to ignore. With attentional bias, you may not even notice all of the available data.

■ *Confirmation bias*—As we mentioned in chapter 4, this is the tendency to look for data that supports your preconceptions. If you read a bad review of a restaurant—but your boss drags you there anyway—you may be naturally inclined to look for more reasons not to like it.[25]

FEELING BETTER YET?

To wrap up, let's look at how some marketers cherry-pick data in ways that make it difficult for the average consumer to see the difference among brands.

Consider the following three statements, which were made by three different health care organizations:

"_____ has been ranked #1 in the nation 22 times."
"_____ is Ranked #1 in More Specialties than any other
    Hospital in the Nation."
"…more physicians from _____ were named to
    America's Top Doctors than from any other hospital in the
    nation."

From reading these statements, it seems that all three of these organizations want you to think that they're the best. But only one can be ranked number one by any given survey or study, assuming there isn't a tie for the top spot.

So what do the others do? They cherry-pick data in order to make the strongest possible claim.[26]

How to Be a Good Consumer of Cherry-Picked Data

How can you spot cherry picking when it's happening to you? Here are five things you can do starting right now:

1. First, when looking at or consuming any statistic, **read the fine print**. In our Gerber example, a lot of information could be gleaned

from the notes and disclaimers. Look closely at caveats, context, and footnotes. When studies are cited—especially by advertisers—you will often find a host of qualifiers, some of which are mandated by the FTC or other agencies. To be a good consumer, pick up a magnifying glass and read the fine print.

2. Second, **think about whether the data was selected in an arbitrary (or nonarbitrary) way**—and whether that might bias the results toward a certain outcome. For example, some of the most frequent apparently arbitrary cuts are found on sports networks. Whenever you hear announcers say, "In the last 19 games..." or "Since 2002..." they're cherry-picking data. Is there a reason to use data from a specific point in time? Perhaps you're only talking about the playoffs, or analyzing a presidential election, or looking at what happened before (or after) an important event, such as a change in a policy. But you need to think about whether the data you're looking at has been selected arbitrarily, or if the way it was selected (by time, etc.) actually has any real meaning.

3. Third, **ask what data might be missing.** In our Gerber example, we saw that there was a large set of pediatricians who didn't recommend any baby food at all. There was another set of pediatricians who didn't recommend any specific brand. Neither of those groups was accurately represented when Gerber made its "four out of five" claim. The numbers that are missing can be just as important as the numbers that are reported. Think about a glass that's half filled with water. An optimist will tell you it's half full. A pessimist will tell you it's half empty. They're both right—and they're both cherry-picking. If you want to make better decisions, you need the full story.

4. Fourth, **don't give more meaning to any one statistic than it deserves.** Think more broadly and don't be swayed by the single number that may appear powerful, but may not accurately represent the whole story because it is based on cherry-picked data. If a Red Sox fan tells his son that Babe Ruth had a record 1,330 strikeouts in his career as a batter, the kid might think that Babe was a lousy player.

5. Finally, it's always good to **ask more questions** about where the data came from. For example, we love coffee. Half of this book was written at coffee shops (we'd need another full page of acknowledgments just for all the friendly baristas). But when you read a report from the National Coffee Association (NCA) quoting the group's president and CEO saying that people are drinking more coffee, you shouldn't be surprised. After all, the core purpose of the NCA "is to champion the well-being of the U.S. coffee industry within the context of the world coffee community."[27] Read any press release from any trade organization, and it's likely to be filled with news that reflects positively on the members of the group. (Although, as the *Washington Post* reported, there was "a study about butter, funded by the butter industry, that found that butter is bad for you."[28]) As always, consider the source when you're consuming your data.

So the next time your boss says you can't have a raise because "sales were down last month," ask her about sales over the past quarter, or year, or decade.

When your 12-year-old wants to see an R-rated movie because "all" of her friends are seeing it, ask if she's including all of her friends in the data set—or just the ones with the cool parents.

And if you ever hear someone say "four out of five people..." it's time to start asking questions.

8

Predicting Disaster

Forecasting the Future

On March 11, 2011, Japan suffered its largest earthquake ever recorded. With a magnitude of 9.0, the Great East Japan Earthquake—centered beneath the Pacific Ocean, not far off Japan's coast—was powerful enough to change the earth's figure axis (the axis around which earth's mass is balanced) by more than half a foot, according to a NASA scientist.[1]

Less than an hour after the earthquake struck, a massive tsunami triggered by the quake reached Japan's Fukushima Daiichi Nuclear Power Plant. The nuclear reactors had automatically shut down upon sensing the earthquake, but the tsunami destroyed emergency generators and cooling pumps, and damaged multiple reactors. As a result, an "enormous amount" of radioactive material was subsequently released into the environment,[2] including millions of gallons of contaminated water reportedly spilled into the ocean.[3]

On the International Nuclear and Radiological Event Scale, the event was ranked a Level 7 accident—the highest possible rating, reserved for major accidents. At the time, Chernobyl was the only other such incident on record. (Not to be overlooked, of course, is the toll that the earthquake and tsunami took on the entire country of Japan, with a reported 15,391 killed, and more than 8,000 missing.[4])

Earthquakes—which often trigger deadly tsunamis—are a known hazard in Japan. Today, a national agency prepares color-coded National Seismic Hazard Maps, which highlight the probability of seismic events throughout the nation.[5] Even when construction at Fukushima was planned, engineers knew about the risk of earthquakes and tsunamis, which is why they designed the plant to withstand a tsunami that was 3.1 meters high. This height was based on the common practice at the time, which was to look at historical tsunami records to determine how tall a future tsunami might be. The 3.1 meter mark was based on a 1960 earthquake that struck off the coast of Chile.[6]

The actual tsunami that hit Fukushima Daiichi was estimated to be 14 to 15 meters tall. The exact height cannot be known, since the gauge that would have measured it was destroyed in the tsunami.

The plant was hit by a natural disaster, but it was the inability to correctly *forecast* a disaster of this magnitude—and then act accordingly—that led to the chain of events. Fukushima was, as the official report of the independent commission noted, "a profoundly manmade disaster—that could and should have been foreseen and prevented."[7]

Other factors certainly played a role. There was alleged "collusion" between Tokyo Electric Power Company (aka TEPCO, the plant operator), regulators, and the government, according to the official report.[8] And some computer models didn't accurately account for how a tsunami can run up the slope of land surrounding a facility, which effectively adds height (above sea level) to the wave. But, at the heart of the matter, a prediction made during the design period had significant consequences decades later.

The original estimate of 3.1 meters was from data recorded just a few years before the plant was designed. But according to the International Atomic Energy Agency, in highly active areas it may be appropriate to study data over "tens of thousands of years."[9] In *Why Fukushima Was Preventable*, a report from the Carnegie Endowment for International Peace, researchers cited one report (published years before the Fukushima incident) that concluded the region "had been inundated by massive tsunamis about once every one thousand years," based on sediment deposits.[10] Another study (published shortly after the 2011 tsunami) that the Carnegie report found listed half a dozen tsunamis in and around Japan that would have had a maximum amplitude of more than 20 meters over the past 500 years.[11] The *New York Times* even reported on the existence of "so-called tsunami stones, some more than six centuries old," inscribed with warnings such as "Do not build your homes below this point!"[12]

In this chapter, we'll explore the role that predictions play in our everyday lives, from earthquakes and coin flips to elections and the weather. And we'll discuss why it's difficult—but certainly not impossible—to predict the future with at least some level of accuracy.

THE SUN WILL COME OUT TOMORROW?

Forecasting is based on a seemingly simple question: Based on the past, can we predict the future?

Except it's not a simple question at all. In fact, it's one of the most complex issues in this book, which is why we've saved it until the end.

Let's start with the first half of the question: "Based on the past..."

If you have all of the past data—what we call the full population—you're off to a good start. For example, if we were somehow able to observe every earthquake and tsunami that has ever hit Japan, we would have data about the full population of these events. (Although even then we would want to think about what else could happen in the future.)

But if we can't gather data about the entire population, we're forced to rely on a sample. And with sampling, we don't always know if it represents the true value in the population or not. So you end up with uncertainty—aka *sampling error*—which we discussed in chapter 5. This is one of the factors behind the Fukushima disaster, where the sample size (a few decades) was arguably too small to be representative of what had happened in the past, given the relative infrequency of potentially catastrophic earthquakes and tsunamis.

The more uncertainty there is in your sample, the more uncertainty there will be in your forecast. A prediction is only as good as the information that goes into it, and in statistics, we call the basis for our forecasts a *model*. The model represents all the inputs—the factors you determine will predict the future outcomes, the underlying sample data you rely upon, and the relationship you apply mathematically. In other words, the model captures how you think various factors relate to one another.

After all, if you can't explain what you've *already* seen, it's difficult—if not impossible—to explain what you *will* see in the future.[13]

Your past data is also subject to many of the factors we've discussed in this book so far—cherry picking, omitted variables, outlier data, statistical significance, etc. Any of these issues in your past data can cause issues with a forecast, because the past data is typically the basis for the future.

Now, when you start to look forward—instead of just back—the problem becomes inherently more complicated because you're combining any uncertainty from the past with uncertainty about the future. What happened yesterday may not happen tomorrow.

For example, let's say you want to predict the price of wheat over the next year. You collect all the data on every wheat price in the history of humankind, and all the different factors that determine the price of wheat (temperature, feed prices, transportation costs, etc.). First, you need to develop a statistical model to determine what factors have affected the price of wheat in the past and how these various factors relate to one another mathematically. Then, based on that model, you predict the price of wheat for next year.[14]

The problem is that no matter how big your sample is (even if it's the full population), and how accurate your statistical model is, there are still unknowns that can cause your forecast to be off:

- What if a railroad strike doubles the transportation costs?
- What if Congress passes new legislation capping the price of wheat?
- What if there's a genetic mutation that makes wheat grow twice as fast, essentially doubling the world's supply?

We don't know that any of these things *will* happen—but we also don't know that they *won't* happen. But these types of intervening events (sometimes called structural changes) interfere with our ability to accurately predict the future based on the past.[15]

Forecasting is difficult because we don't know everything about how the world works. There are unforeseen events. Unknown processes. Random occurrences. People are unpredictable, and things don't always stay the same. The data you're studying can change—as can your understanding of the underlying process. (With Fukushima, for example, the predicted tsunami height was raised from 3.1 meters to 5.7 meters based on new methodology proposed by the Japan Society of Civil Service Engineers.[16]) These are some of the considerations you need to keep in mind when thinking about forecasts.

CHOOSE YOUR WORDS CAREFULLY

An earthquake can't be predicted. At least, not according to the U.S. Geological Survey (USGS), which draws a sharp distinction between predictions and forecasts. "There is no scientifically plausible way of predicting the occurrence of a particular earthquake," they note, adding that "prediction, as people expect it, requires predicting the magnitude, timing, and location of the future earthquake, which is not currently possible."[17] We simply don't have the data, nor do we have the technology, to accurately predict quakes at this time.

That said, the USGS does describe the places "most likely to produce earthquakes in the long term." They call this forecasting, when they estimate the likelihood of a seismic event occurring over a period of time.

This brings us to the distinction—or lack thereof—between a *prediction* and a *forecast*. As Nate Silver notes in *The Signal and the Noise*, the terms are used differently by some (most notably seismologists, who study earthquakes) but interchangeably by others. Some would argue that predictions are binary—something will or won't happen—while forecasts are more probabilistic—there's an X percent chance that something will happen. (To further complicate the issue, an *estimate* may be used when talking about past, current, or future data.)

We recognize that these types of distinctions exist for certain applications. For our purposes, however, we're generally going to treat "prediction" and "forecast" synonymously unless noted otherwise.

Why?

First of all, because this is a book for the everyday consumer of data, not necessarily for seismologists or advanced statisticians.

And second, because we don't want something that is essentially a semantic distinction to overshadow the point of this chapter, which is to illustrate the ways in which you should—and shouldn't—use data to determine what may happen in the future.

CHARGING AHEAD

Did your credit card company ever call you because it thought your card was stolen? It happens all the time. You go on vacation to Europe or take a big shopping trip to the outlet mall, and all of a sudden you get a call from the credit card company because it's concerned about fraudulent activity on your card.

Why?

Probably because the company is looking at the past data and using that to model your future purchasing behavior. And when the data doesn't fit the model, you get a call. (On its website, Visa even suggests that you tell your financial institution if you'll be traveling, which can "help ensure that your card isn't flagged for unusual activity."[18]) This is a perfect example of a *false positive*—the credit card company predicted that the charges on your card were potentially fraudulent, but it was wrong.

Events like this, which may not be accounted for in the statistical model, are potential sources of *prediction error*. Just as sampling error tells us about the uncertainty in our sample, prediction error is a way to measure uncertainty in the future, essentially by comparing the predicted results to the actual outcomes, once they occur.[19]

Prediction error is often measured using a *prediction interval*, which is the range in which we expect to see the next data point. When the credit card company calls you about your "stolen" credit card, it could be because your latest purchase was outside its prediction interval.[20] So, by calling Visa and letting the company know you're going on vacation to Hawaii, you're essentially expanding its prediction interval to include mai tais on the beach.

You probably know—at least intuitively—that forecasts often become more accurate as you get closer to an event. Statistically, what's happening here is that your prediction error and prediction intervals are shrinking. Imagine it's May 1, and you're trying to forecast your company's sales for next month, versus trying to forecast sales for the rest of the year. Your forecast for next month will likely have less prediction error (and a smaller prediction interval) for two reasons:

1. You have more—and more recent—historical sample data. If you try to determine on May 1 what your year-end sales will be, you only have four months' of present-year data. If you wait until October 1, you have nine months' of data for that year. All things being equal, more historical data typically allows you to make a more accurate forecast.

2. Similarly, there are (theoretically) fewer unforeseen events that could happen between May 1 and June 1, versus things that could happen between May 1 and December 31. The more time you have, the more opportunity for factors that could affect your forecast (new competition, a different regulatory environment, changes in vendor pricing, etc.).

Just keep in mind that prediction error is not the same as sampling error. We see this confusion in political polls, which often talk about a margin of error as if it were simply a sampling issue. But sampling more people—even the whole population—won't completely eliminate the prediction error. Support for political candidates changes over time. Some candidates gain support as their rivals drop out, while others lose potential voters following a poor debate performance, or perhaps a mistimed yell at a rally (aka the "Dean Scream").[21]

Finally, let's talk about *forecast bias*, which is the term used to describe a prediction error that is consistently high (a positive forecast bias) or low (a negative bias). Why does this happen? Perhaps there is an error with the model that you're using. For example, if you run the local water utility and you're trying to forecast the annual demand for water with a model that doesn't account for the fact that your town is growing by 5,000 people each year, you're likely going to have a negative forecast bias—it's always going to be low. Of course, forecast bias can also be intentional. Imagine that you run a division of a company, and that your allocated budget for next year is based on your forecast. The higher your forecast, the more money your division will get. With this type of incentive in place, it's easy to see how forecast bias can occur—something to keep in mind if your job entails asking people for their forecasts.

GREAT EXPECTATIONS

"The right way to view forecasting," said Jeffrey Brown—a professor at the University of Illinois, and director of the Center for Business and Public Policy in the College of Business, whom we interviewed—"is as a way to narrow down the range of possible outcomes from 'anything can happen' to 'here is a range of likely outcomes.'"

But here's the issue—according to Brown (who is also associate director of the NBER Retirement Research Center, which informs policy makers), "politicians and the public tend to be much less focused on uncertainty, and just want a simple narrative, such as 'the Social Security system is going bankrupt' or 'Social Security will be just fine.'"

There is uncertainty around any estimate. But that's not what some people want to hear—they just want a number.

As Brown explained, "most economists understand that what we are really doing is making 'projections' rather than 'predictions.' In other words, we can be reasonably comfortable in modeling how the system's finances will evolve *if* fertility or mortality or labor force participation evolves in a particular way. But we are much less comfortable stating with any certainty that fertility or mortality or labor force participation *will* move in a particular way."

But unless someone has been trained in statistics (or has read this book!) these types of subtleties and nuances may not mean much to them. "As a result," noted Brown, "we often see situations in which people express surprise or disappointment or even anger when a policy does not have exactly the predicted effect, even in cases where the outcome is well within the confidence interval that would have applied to the initial estimate."

HEADS I WIN, TAILS YOU LOSE

Many of the forecasts we have discussed so far are *deterministic:* forecasts in which you determine a *precise* outcome. For example: "It is going to rain today." This is similar to the way in which seismologists use the word "prediction" (a magnitude 3.1 earthquake will hit north of San Francisco on March 2).

Determining whether a flipped coin will land heads up or tails up is a classic example of a *probabilistic forecast.* A probabilistic forecast is one in which you determine the probability of an outcome. For example: "The chance of rain today is 20 percent." This is similar to the way in which seismologists use the word "forecast."

When you flip a coin, you know it's going to land one way or the other. (Yes, there is a possibility it can land on its edge. But given that one paper calculated that probability as 1 in 6,000, we're going to ignore that for now, and—for the purposes of this section—assume a coin can only land heads up or tails up.[22] We're also going to assume, as an article from *American Statistician* noted, that "it is *not* possible to bias a coin flip" to make it substantially more likely to land heads versus tails.[23] And we're going to flip it—not spin it—since a spinning penny, for example, "will land as tails about 80 percent of the time" because its center of mass is shifted toward the heads side, according to an article in *Science News Online.*[24])

So, taking our flipped, non-weighted, non-edge-landing coin, we know the following:

The probability of the coin landing heads up is 50 percent.
The probability of the coin landing tails up is also 50 percent.

If you flip the coin twice, the probability of getting one heads and one tails is 50 percent.

But here's where it gets interesting.

If you flip the coin 10 times, the probability of getting 5 heads and 5 tails isn't 50 percent. It's actually just under 25 percent.

If you flip the coin 100 times, the probability of getting 50 heads and 50 tails is approximately 8 percent.

Huh?

What you're seeing here is the difference between what *should* happen (in theory) and what actually *does* happen, in real life. The coin doesn't know that it's supposed to land heads up half the time and tails up the other half. This is an important lesson about forecasting—just because something is the most likely outcome doesn't mean it *will* actually happen.

(Many people also get confused by coin flips because they think, for example, if you flip a coin twice there's a one-third chance of getting two heads, one-third chance of getting two tails, and one-third chance of getting one heads and one tails. But because there are *two* ways to get one heads and one tails—heads on coin A and tails on coin B versus the opposite—there's actually a one-quarter chance of getting two heads, one-quarter chance of getting two tails, and one-half chance of getting one heads and one tails. Remember to consider *all* of the outcomes when you're developing your forecast.)

The more coins you flip, of course, the closer your results should be to a 50–50 split. Why? Because by flipping the coin more times, you're essentially taking a larger sample size of an infinite number of coin flips. And a larger sample size—assuming all else is equal—is going to give you more accurate results than a smaller sample size. (Although even a large sample size isn't a guarantee. In 1936, *Literary Digest* received approximately 2.3 *million* responses to a survey, and predicted that Alfred Landon would get 57 percent of the vote for U.S. president, thereby defeating Franklin D. Roosevelt. In reality, Roosevelt received more than 60 percent of the vote.)

Now, remember when we talked about using past data to forecast the future? This is one of those instances in which past data doesn't matter. That's because we know that a coin flip (at least the way we've described it) is a truly random event. And with a truly random event, you can't use the past as a model.

If you flip a coin 10 times and it comes up heads every time, there's still a 50 percent chance the next one will be heads. Even if you flip it

100 times, 1,000 times, or 1 million times and it comes up heads every time, there's still a 50 percent chance the next one will be heads because we have a known model, in which a coin lands heads up half the time and tails up the other half.

A lot of people don't understand this. Intuitively, they think the next one has to be tails. But statistically, they're absolutely wrong. Yes, it's unlikely that you're going to get 10 heads in a row. But that still has nothing to do with the future. A 50–50 split should happen over time, but each flip of the coin is an independent event, completely separate from what happened in the past.[25]

This is known as the gambler's fallacy—thinking you're going to win after a streak of losses. "But in reality," according to research done at Texas A&M, "your odds of winning are no different than they were before."[26] (The good news is, it may not be your fault. The researchers developed a model of neurons in your brain, and found that "the neurons that preferred alternating patterns such as head–tail significantly outnumbered the neurons that preferred repeating patterns such as head–head." Fascinating stuff. Just keep in mind that it was based on a *model* of neurons, not actual neurons.)

As a smart consumer of data, you need to watch out for the gambler's fallacy when you're analyzing forecasts. Ask yourself: Is the forecast built from a model in which the past data matters? Or is it forecasting events that are completely independent from the past?[27]

We'll leave you with this quote from *Lotto Stats* magazine, which actually stated, "The more information you have in front of you, the better your chances of winning when playing the Daily Numbers Games."[28]

Cover your ears, kids, because we're calling bullshit on this one.

THE FORTUNE-TELLERS AMONG US

People around the world have long claimed the power to predict the future, from Nostradamus supposedly foreseeing the Great Fire of London, to modern-day prophet wannabes claiming, "The end is near!" Even on stage, soothsayers have played pivotal roles, warning Oedipus that he would kill his father (and marry his mother) and beseeching Julius Caesar to "beware the Ides of March."

Today, there are still men and women whose livelihood depends on their ability to be right about the future.

But they're not soothsayers, prophets, or oracles.

In this case, they're hedge fund managers.

Hedge funds are investments that pool money from multiple investors. They use flexible investment strategies to earn returns, and are often found in the portfolios of wealthier investors. That's because you typically need to be a "qualified purchaser," "qualified client," or "accredited investor"—basically, to have a net worth in excess of $1 million—to invest in a hedge fund under U.S. federal securities laws. (Of course, even if you aren't rich, there's still a good chance that you have an interest in hedge funds. For example, if you're a state employee or retiree in Texas, approximately 5 percent of your pension funds may be invested in hedge funds.[29])

A hedge fund manager's job—like that of most investors—is to predict what happens next. He has to buy and sell investments in accordance with the goals of the hedge fund. (And yes, it's usually he, even though female hedge fund managers have outperformed men, according to at least one study.[30])

The problem is that a prediction is only as good as the data it's built on.

"The idea that you can draw conclusions based on 10 years of returns is one of the biggest fallacies in Wall Street, in my opinion," said Neal Berger, founder and president of Eagle's View Capital Management—a hedge fund of funds—when we interviewed him.[31] (A hedge fund of funds is a fund that invests in multiple hedge funds, just like a mutual fund invests in multiple equities.) "Even going back 100 years is not statistically relevant to truly draw a normal distribution curve," added Berger. "We don't have enough data in the entire history of markets as to what could happen."

Of course, when talking about hedge funds and forecasting, it's interesting to note that these funds (perhaps because of management fees and other costs typically associated with them) don't always provide better returns than the market. As a *Bloomberg Business* headline noted,

"Hedge Funds Trail Stocks for Fifth Year with 7.4% Return."[32] This may be a classic case of cherry picking, however, as looking at other time periods produces very different results—including a *Wall Street Journal* article that noted, "Over the past 15 years, [hedge funds'] returns have beaten the overall stock market."[33] And, to be fair, outperforming the S&P 500 (a constantly changing list of approximately 500 stocks) in terms of nominal returns may not be the goal of all hedge funds, as Berger and others have noted. Rather, the ultimate objective is often to provide the best risk-adjusted returns—a measure that factors in the risk that was taken in order to achieve the returns. Although sometimes, the predictions are off. In one classic example, hedge fund Long-Term Capital Management (LTCM) "lost $4.4 billion of its $4.7 billion in capital" in less than one year, in part due to spreads that didn't converge as predicted.[34]

Regardless of their performance, hedge funds sometimes get a bad rap because of the salaries that some hedge fund managers earn. *Institutional Investor's Alpha* publishes an annual "rich list" in which it estimates the earnings of the top managers. Even on the 2015 list, which highlighted the group's *worst* year in nearly a decade, the 25 people on the list "made a paltry $11.62 billion combined." That's half of what they made the year before, in case you want to feel sorry for them (although with a median salary of $400 million that's hard to do).[35]

Apparently, the right type of forecasting can pay pretty well.

Of course, you don't have to be a hedge fund manager to benefit from forecasting. For example, as economist J. J. Prescott explained in an interview, negotiations often rely heavily on predictions. "In negotiation," notes Prescott, " 'BATNA' (the best alternative to the negotiated agreement) is really the most important thing to know. If the other party has good outside options (like going to trial), then settling in a satisfactory way is going to be tough. Thus, in settlement negotiations, you not only need to predict your best alternative option, but also determine what your counterpart is likely to view as his or her best alternative."

Thinking about how a decision will affect you—and your colleagues, counterparts, and competition—may help give you an edge at the office.

WHAT DO YOU KNOW?

A coin flip is an event with a known outcome. You can make all the predictions you want, but you know that the outcome is limited to one of three options: heads, tails, or (if you're going to be technical) edge.

Many forecasts will fall within a known range, simply because of the way they are measured. For example, you have a limited number of options if you try to forecast:

- Who will win the World Series
- Your end-of-semester calculus grade at the beginning of the school year
- Whether your opponent will choose rock, paper, or scissors

On the other hand, with some forecasts you're dealing with a much larger number of possible outcomes—perhaps even infinite possibilities. For example, you have a much wider range of outcomes if you try to forecast:

- Who will be president of the United States in 50 years
- What song the radio station will play next
- Your job title a decade from now (considering that some future jobs may not even exist today)

If you can limit the number of outcomes, your forecast may change significantly, and you may be able to reduce your prediction error. We see this every year as Major League Baseball teams are eliminated from the playoffs. With each team that gets knocked out, the probability of each remaining team winning the World Series will most likely increase. Just as a forecast with a shorter time frame may be more accurate (all things being equal), in some cases you may be able to produce better forecasts by limiting the number of potential outcomes. But, even sometimes when we only have two possible outcomes, skilled pollsters can get it wrong.

THE TRUMAN STORY

By most accounts, Thomas Dewey should have been our 34th president.

It was 1948, and the major polls predicted a sweeping victory for Dewey, the governor of New York. But the polls were wrong. Instead of sending Dewey to the White House, the voters elected Harry Truman by nearly five points.

The landmark event led to one of the most memorable media mistakes of the century when the *Chicago Daily Tribune* printed nearly 150,000 papers with the erroneous headline, "Dewey Defeats Truman."[36]

So what happened? Why were the polls wrong?

First of all, the pollsters stopped polling "a few weeks too soon," according to George Gallup Jr. (cochair of the Gallup polling organization at the time), quoted in the *LA Times*.[37] Pollsters didn't think there would be major changes in opinion during the final weeks leading up to the campaign—but there were, as Truman supporters rallied the labor vote. (Meanwhile, overconfident Dewey supporters "played golf that day," noted pollster Burns W. "Bud" Roper.)[38]

Another factor was that the polling models were built on past elections, which differed in many ways from the 1948 contest. At the time, every presidential election going back to 1932—a span of 16 years—had included (and been won by) Franklin Roosevelt. In each one of these elections, Roosevelt had defeated one main opponent. Fast-forward to 1948—a race without Roosevelt, and with *four* major contenders (Dewey, Truman, Strom Thurmond, and Henry Wallace).[39]

In this case, the newspaper made a deterministic forecast by proclaiming that Dewey would win. But the data from the polls apparently didn't account for the latest voter sentiments, and the statistical models of the time seem to have been built around two-person races. And that's how we ended up with what *Time* magazine said is "generally regarded as the greatest upset in American political history."[40]

COINCIDENCE AND PROBABILITY

As always, it's important to pay attention to exactly how the data is used. For example, saying there's a 100 percent chance of having pizza tonight versus a 100 percent chance of having pizza next week are two very different things, statistically speaking. With the former, you know you're going to have pizza one out of one nights. With the latter, you may have pizza every night—or you may only get it one out of the seven nights.

Although some people use them interchangeably, probability and odds are *not* the same and people often misuse the terms. Probability is the likelihood that an outcome will occur. The odds of something happening, statistically speaking, is the ratio of favorable outcomes to unfavorable outcomes.

Picture a standard deck of 52 cards.

The *probability* that you'll pull a face card (a Jack, Queen, or King) is 23 percent. There are 12 of these cards in the deck, and 12 divided by 52 is 23 percent.

The *odds* of pulling a face card are 12:40 (there are 12 face cards and 40 non-face cards).

Probability and odds are related—and you can calculate either one from the other—but they're not the same.

You may also hear the word "risk" when talking about future events. Risk is another one of those tricky terms that can mean different things to different people—especially if you're in the investment or insurance industries. But, in general, risk takes into account not only the probability of an event, but also the consequences.

So, for example, Mike knows how to juggle. When he juggles apples, there is a 1 percent probability that he will make a mistake and drop one on his toe. When he juggles knives, there is also a 1 percent probability that he will make a mistake and drop one on his toe. The probabilities are the same—but the risk is very different. (For a fascinating/terrifying article on catastrophe risk—and to learn how underestimating hurricane damage nearly bankrupted the U.S. insurance industry—read the *New York Times Magazine* article "In Nature's Casino."[41])

Just because an event has a low probability of occurring doesn't mean it won't happen. In an *Atlantic* article, the editor of *Flying* magazine said the FAA standard for certain components is "one in a billion probability of failure, or 10 to the minus 9th. The FAA calls this standard 'improbable.'"[42] But it's not impossible. In fact, if the statistics are done correctly, it's actually *probable* that a one in a billion event will occur once out of every billion occurrences. This is the reason that—as Berger noted—a casino wouldn't let Bill Gates come in and put $5 billion on one bet. "If they're the most unlucky people in the world, it bankrupts them."

Especially when you start looking at large data sets, you can expect to see these low-probability events. As the *Wall Street Journal* noted in an article about coincidences in lottery drawings, "with millions of people choosing numbers in hundreds of lotteries around the world each week, coincidences are bound to happen."[43]

Consider the black swan. A few hundred years ago, people assumed that the existence of a black swan was impossible, simply because they hadn't seen any evidence of one before. But not seeing a black swan doesn't mean it doesn't exist, just that we haven't seen it—yet. Today, a "black swan" event is something that is highly improbable, yet has a massive impact when it occurs; the term was popularized by Nassim Nicholas Taleb, who has written extensively about the topic of uncertainty. Just because it hasn't happened yet doesn't mean it can't—or won't—happen. Black swans exist.[44]

ARE YOU SURE?

So far, we've focused primarily on statistical concepts. But there are certainly many psychological factors that can play a role in forecasting. For example:

- Overconfidence—A paper for the *Journal of Finance* found that high trading levels (which can sometimes be explained by overconfidence) can result in poor financial performance; during a period when the market returned nearly 18 percent, those who traded the most earned less than 12 percent.[45]

■ Fear—The chance of being killed by a shark is 1 in 3.7 million, according to *The Week* magazine.[46] But when you're at the beach with your family and friends, it can be hard to think logically— and forecast accurately—when you keep hearing the music from *Jaws* in your head.

■ Idiosyncratic rater effect—As a *Harvard Business Review* article noted, ratings of people are actually driven by the person *doing* the rating, not by the person being rated; on average, the article found, "61% of my rating of you is a reflection of me."[47]

Predicting the future isn't always easy. (Maybe that's why those telephone psychics charge so much.) Focus groups for the *Seinfeld* pilot said it was "weak," yet the show went on to be one of the most-watched series of all time.[48] Statistics play a key role. But overconfidence, fear, and plain old human nature are just a few of the nonstatistical factors that can affect a forecast. Keep an eye out for them, and you'll be better off for it.

How to Be a Good Consumer of Forecasts

Forecasts are all around you, from the time you wake up and see the weather forecast on your smartphone to the moment you watch the latest election poll on the nightly news. Here are five things you can do to understand forecasts, starting right now:

1. First of all, know that **predicting the future depends on knowing the past (or knowing the model)**. If there are statistical concerns with the past data or the model—sampling errors, omitted variables, miscalculated averages, structural changes, etc.—those issues are going to manifest themselves in the forecast.

2. Secondly, there are different types of forecasts—specifically, **deterministic forecasts versus probabilistic forecasts**. When you're

looking at a forecast, understand what type it is. Does it say that it will rain during your golf tournament tomorrow (deterministic)? Or that there's a 40 percent probability that you'll be rained out (probabilistic)?

3. Next, **understand the terminology**. A forecast and a prediction are often synonymous—but not always. When people use words like "likelihood" or "chances" or "risk" or "odds," you need to know what they're talking about. The same word can mean something very different to an economist versus a seismologist, or a pollster versus an insurance executive.

4. Understand that **the accuracy of a forecast may change over time**. Forecasting a baseball game's final score in the seventh inning is likely to be more accurate than forecasting it in the first inning, because you have more data available. Forecasts may also become more accurate as new technology and methodology for gathering data and building statistical models are developed. Just think about all the recent advances in genomic medicine that give us the ability to make predictions about our long-term health. That said, you have fewer opportunities to change your forecast, the closer you get to the forecast event.

5. Finally, accept that **there may always be some level of uncertainty**. As Neal Berger (the hedge fund guy) said, "We have to operate in a world where we're never going to have 100 percent surety or comfort. It's hard for people to reconcile that we're living in an unpredictable world. A lot of people can't get their head around that, and want to think life is going to be normal every day. But we can't mitigate every possible risk. We have to make the best judgments we can."

In the immortal words of Yogi Berra, "It is tough to make predictions, especially about the future."

9

It's a Jungle Out There

Putting It All Together

Imagine going to the zoo and seeing a lion. In the next cage over, there's an elephant. Another exhibit holds the giraffes. And so on. Each animal is in its own contained area, with a nice little sign that tells you more about it.

That's sort of the approach we've taken with this book, explaining one statistical concept at a time, each one with its own separate chapter.

Now, it's time to go on safari.

In the real world, statistical issues rarely exist in isolation. You're going to come across cases where there's more than one problem with the data. For example, just because you identify some sampling errors doesn't mean there aren't also issues with cherry picking and correlations and averages and forecasts—or simply more sampling issues, for that matter. Some cases may have no statistical issues, some may have dozens. But you need to keep your eyes open in order to spot them all.

That's what this chapter is all about.

Here, you'll find a few of our favorite studies and stories that show how multiple statistical concepts can affect the way that data is distributed, consumed, and interpreted.

Here we go.

SHOW ME THE MONEY

An article in the *Atlantic* asked the question, "Why Do Former High School Athletes Make More Money?"[1] According to the piece, people who were athletes in high school end up with "higher status careers" compared to those who weren't, with wages "between 5 and 15 percent higher than those of the poor trombonists and Yearbook Club presidents."

Nice. As if the kids who played trombone in high school didn't have it bad enough already.

This article struck Mrs. Everydata (John's wife) as exactly the type of question that raised a flag for sound consumers of data, and at her urging, we investigated the study and the underlying numbers.

The basic premise of the article is based on studies by researchers at Cornell and Southern Illinois University who looked at two unique data sets on biodata.[2] In psychology, biodata is self-reported data about one's self (i.e., "biographical data"). There are two studies—in the first one, a sample of 66 adults participated in a survey about leadership traits and past experience in extracurrriculars. This part of the survey was to capture subjective views about participation in athletics, and asked about how a person's extracurricular activities related to qualities such as self-confidence, leadership, and self-respect.

From this small sample of 66 people, the authors conclude that "people tend to expect former student-athletes to demonstrate greater leadership ability as well as organizationally beneficial personality traits; however, former student athletes are not expected to be altruistic with respect to others." We won't spend a lot of time on the first study, other than to say there is always controversy about these types of attitudinal surveys across fields (economists tend to be very skeptical, but those in industrial organizational psychology utilize them quite often). From a statistical standpoint, however, it does appear that the key result may be affected by combining all sports activities into one bucket, and all non-sports activities into a second bucket.

That said, let's focus on the second study, which conducted a statistical analysis of the 2000 University of Illinois Veteran's Survey.

According to the study, this sample contained information on 931 World War II veterans who were ages 71 to 93 at the time of completion of the survey in 2000. The key conclusion from the authors here is that participation in sports as a kid has a positive effect that "persist[s] for more than 55 years." The authors describe "a positive relationship between participation in competitive youth sports and several measures of long-term personal success and prosociality."

Here are a few observations:

First, there is no part of either study one or study two that looks at or measures the *actual effect* of high school sports on wages. That data does not exist. Rather, the study looks at how *self-reported data* of participating in a college sport 55 years ago *correlates* with leadership metrics, and with trade jobs versus upper-management jobs. This is a fairly inexact methodology by which to measure whether one gets a better job.

Second, the premise of the study is that sports participation more than 55 years ago correlates with future job outcomes. But there is only a somewhat limited set of explanatory variables; in fact, the only other explanations that the study can control for are age and size of hometown. This immediately raises the question of *omitted variables*—what if high school sports participation by a subset of male veterans ages 71 to 93 was correlated with any number of other factors, such as their benefits under the GI Bill, their education level, their participation in World War II, or their ability? This is a classic issue in many studies of job performance.

Finally, the authors of the veterans study also note their results are potentially picking up correlations but no causation. There are a lot of two-way analyses in this study—leadership correlated with athletics, self-confidence correlated with self-respect, etc. Here is one possible explanation: What if kids who have time for sports are better off financially (i.e., they don't have to work after school)? Being better off financially when you are young could explain success later in life. The point is, this is a complicated question, and it is highly unlikely that these particular metrics are capturing a true causal relationship.

We don't mind biometric data—and the study is certainly very interesting. But this is yet another example where the data captured in the headlines can't quite convey the nuanced interpretation of the underlying study.

LAW AND ORDER

"How much money does it take to make a lawyer happy?"

It's not a joke. It's the headline of an article from *Law360* regarding its Lawyer Satisfaction Survey.

So seriously, how much are we talking about? The answer? Half a million dollars a year.

It turns out that lawyers who made more than $500,000 are happier at work and less likely to leave for another firm, according to *Law360*. As the article noted, "While happiness is not directly tied to salary at every pay grade, $500,000 appears to be a threshold above which lawyers consider themselves either 'satisfied' or 'very satisfied' with all aspects of their jobs."[3]

In a flurry of stories tied to the survey, *Law360* also found that:

- Employment attorneys are the happiest
- Non-equity partners are "the most miserable"[4]
- Lawyers at big firms (more than 500 people) are happier than those at small firms

These findings make for great headlines, and will surely cause some hand-wringing in glass-walled law firm conference rooms from D.C. to Dallas.

But before you get too worked up about it, let's take a closer look at what this data really means.

There are more than 1.3 million lawyers in the U.S.[5] This survey is based on responses from 300 of them. But it's the makeup of the sample that concerns us more than the sample size. Because the results appear to be based on a self-selected group of attorneys who responded to the survey, according to the *Law360* articles. When you have a group of people opting into a study, there's an opportunity for *selection bias*. The results may be biased toward those who chose to participate. Are the attorneys who responded any different from those who were too busy to answer, or chose not to respond for whatever reason—and would those differences be related to the survey's findings? For example, is it possible that non-equity partners who are happy are also the busiest, and therefore didn't have time to respond to the survey? It's certainly possible.

It's also possible that the attorneys misrepresented their happiness, inflated their salaries, and gave all sorts of false information on the survey, since it was *self-reported data*. Do we have any proof that they did this? Nope. But with this type of survey, there aren't always safeguards in place to prevent misleading (or flat-out wrong) responses. Self-reported data itself isn't necessarily the concern; the issue is that we may get the wrong answer to a question because self-reported data is subject to manipulation.

Let's move on to the employment attorneys, who *Law360* said are happier than non-employment attorneys. But employment attorneys— at least the ones who responded to this survey—also earn less than non-employment attorneys. Given that salary is supposedly tied to happiness, perhaps there are other variables at play here? Or maybe people who go into employment law are just naturally more optimistic. What are the *omitted variables*? We don't know—and that's an issue.

We also don't know if money really does "make a lawyer happy," as the aforementioned headline states, implying a *causal relationship* when we haven't seen evidence that it's anything more than a *correlation*. In fact, in another story, *Law360* noted that "happiness is not entirely cash-driven," which raises the possibility that there are factors other than money that drive happiness.[6]

Here's another issue—lack of context. If you read all the articles, you might learn that one group of attorneys is 17 percent more satisfied than another, or 32 percent more likely to stay at their firm, and so on. But *Law360* doesn't appear to give enough detail about its *methodology* to know what these results mean. Were attorneys asked to rank their satisfaction on a numeric scale of 1 to 5 (or perhaps 1 to 100 or some other range)? Were they given choices such as "dissatisfied," "satisfied," and "extremely satisfied"? Having more information about the methodology could provide more insight in terms of what the survey results actually mean—and may reveal any bias in the methodology.

Law360 is certainly not alone in issuing these types of results. We've seen similar types of surveys from the computer industry, the architecture and engineering industries, and many others. And we're not saying that we expect statistical rigor in these types of articles. But the issues we've raised here are just a few of the things you may want to think about as you read your e-mails, scan news alerts on your smartphone, and take in all of the data that surrounds you at work—and at home.

HAPPY BIRTH DAY TO YOU?

"Astrology may be bogus, but the month you're born really seems to matter for your health," said the *Washington Post*.[7]

Seriously?

We agree with the astrology is bogus part. But can when you're born truly affect your health?

The first thing you want to do is consider whether the study was *misinterpreted* by the media. We've certainly seen this before—instances in which a scientific paper explored a correlation, which was then turned into implied causation by the media. In this case, however, the *Post's* reporting (as usual) seemed legit. The article was careful to explain that the time of year you're born has "a connection with the diseases" you may face later in life. And when we went to the original study in the *Journal of the American Medical Informatics Association*, the content confirmed what we saw in the *Post*. "An individual's birth month," the study noted, "has a significant impact on the diseases they develop during their lifetime."[8]

Okay, so then the next step is to try to figure out why there could be a relationship between birth month and disease. Let's start—as we often do—by examining the *sample*. While the researchers looked at the records of 1.75 million people (a seemingly adequate sample size), they were only taken from patients treated at New York Presbyterian Hospital/Columbia University Medical Center in Manhattan. Needless to say, Manhattan isn't representative of New York City, let alone the U.S. as a whole—or the larger global population. For example, only 1 percent of the patients were identified as Asian (although there could have been more in the "Other" and "Unidentified" categories, which made up nearly half of the sample).

So, is it possible that something in the sample could explain the link between birth month and disease? What if all that confetti in Times

Square on New Year's Eve causes asthma, which was one of the health issues linked to birth month? This is where you need to consider the existence of *omitted variables*. In other words, is birth month the reason that some people have higher incidences of disease? Or is the birth month simply correlated with disease, while something else is truly the causal factor? For example, as the authors note, there are seasonal factors (allergens, exposure to sunlight, etc.) that may play a role.

What else should you consider as a smart consumer of data? Here's an interesting observation—in their study, the researchers found 55 diseases that were "significantly dependent" on birth month. That's a considerable number when you look at it in isolation. But the researchers examined data for 1,688 different diseases, which means they only found a link to birth month in approximately 3 percent of the diseases they studied. Sometimes, the more data you study, the more likely you are to find a result that is *statistically significant*, given that significance typically measures the probability of a relationship. Were any of these relationships between birth month and disease due to random chance? Some p-values were less than .001, while others were considerably higher. This type of result is a likely candidate for the multiple comparison problem we discussed earlier.

So now we're left with the question: What do we do with this data? Well, let's look at the *magnitude* (size) of the effect. In some cases, the birth month might relate to a roughly 5 percent increased risk of a disease, or perhaps an overall lifespan shortened (or lengthened) by four to five months.[9] Is that enough to be concerned with?

Finally, let's consider what impact this data could have on your life. The 55 diseases cited by the researchers all have differing effects on people's lives. Asthma, for example, may be treatable with medication and lifestyle changes, while some of the cardiovascular conditions (such as congestive cardiac failure) may need to be managed more closely and intensively. Beyond the individual health concerns, how would you use these findings to determine when to have a baby? If you were dating someone, would you ask when the person's birthday is, to screen out potentially unhealthy suitors? Like many studies, this one raises a number of questions not just in terms of the statistical impact of the data, but also of the economic impact on our lives.

TOO COOL FOR SCHOOL

Even in middle school, kids know who the "cool kids" are. They're the ones watching R-rated movies, shoplifting snacks from the local convenience store, maybe smoking cigarettes (or something a bit more potent) behind the school.

But these teenage troublemakers will grow out of it, right? Isn't there hope for middle school punks? Or does your behavior at 13 truly predict where you'll be at 23?

If you're the parent of a teenage delinquent, you may want to skip this next section. Because researchers have found that pseudomature behaviors (kids trying to act older than they are) in early adolescents "predicted long-term difficulties in close relationships, as well as significant problems with alcohol and substance use, and elevated levels of criminal behavior."[10]

Yikes.

The study—the first we've seen to name-drop Shakespeare, James Dean, and Tina Fey in the first paragraph—was published in *Child Development* and subsequently covered in a number of media outlets, which isn't surprising given the eyebrow-raising subject matter. In a press release, the professor who led the study tried to explain the link between early behavior and later consequences, theorizing that cool kids "needed more and more extreme behaviors to try to appear cool" as time went on.[11]

Now if you're a parent, you may read this study and want to lock your kids in their rooms until they're 30. But as a consumer of data, you may look at this case study from a few other angles.

For example, you may wonder how the teens were chosen—aka *sampled*—from the full population. Researchers studied public school kids from suburban and urban areas in the Southeastern U.S. whose families said they were interested in the study. Do these same results apply to kids who are homeschooled, or go to private schools? Would we find the same behavior patterns in kids outside the Southeast? Do kids in rural areas act differently? What about kids whose families weren't interested in participating? In this case, we don't have the data to know for sure how the results would have differed.

In half a dozen areas throughout the study, the authors spoke of ways in which data was *averaged*. For example, the researchers took data about alcohol use from multiple years and averaged it to provide an overall drug use score. (And yes, the data was, in some cases, *self-reported*.)

The study also highlights another issue to watch out for—using a forecast from *one* sample set on a *different* sample set or population. This happens sometimes when the media covers these types of studies. For example, one media outlet (which will remain unnamed for its protection) used a headline noting how behavior in middle school can affect "your future." It's a subtle shift, but now instead of talking about how the behavior of 184 teens predicted *their* future, the article is speaking to *you*, the reader.

When a media report or an original study starts ascribing findings to people (or other subjects) outside the sample set, that's saying something about *external validity*—which is a way we measure whether the results apply beyond the sample. Sometimes they do, sometimes they don't—but it's something you need to watch for, especially when you're reading the news.

SOLD ON DATA

If you're trying to buy or sell a home, you've probably heard of Zillow. With a database of more than 110 million homes in the U.S., Zillow lets you see how much nearly any home in the country is worth.[12]

Well, sort of.

Here's how it works: when you look up a home, you'll see a "Zestimate," which is Zillow's beautifully branded name for a home's estimated market value.

To come up with the Zestimate, Zillow uses a proprietary formula that relies on both public and user-reported data. According to its website, the company looks at all sorts of data, including:

- Square footage
- Location
- Number of bedrooms and bathrooms

- Property tax data
- Past sale prices
- Comparable sales of other homes in the same area

In fact, you can probably look up your home right now on Zillow and see how much the company thinks it's worth—even if you bought it years ago.

If there's not enough data for a Zestimate, sometimes Zillow simply doesn't give one. For example, when we looked at Zillow's data, none of the homes in Vermont had a Zestimate.[13] Zero. Zip. Zilch. If you live in New Jersey, however, you're in luck—Zillow has a Zestimate for 99.4 percent of the homes in the Garden State.

Even though Zillow points out that a Zestimate is not an appraisal, many people still rely on it when buying or selling a house. "If a house for sale has a Zestimate of $350,000, a buyer might challenge the sellers' list price of $425,000," noted a *Los Angeles Times* article.[14] Similarly, sellers might ask an agent why they should list their house for far below the Zestimate.[15]

"Not a week goes by that we don't encounter a consumer who is fixated on a particular value for a home because that's what Zillow says it is," said an officer of a real estate agency in a piece for the *Washington Post*, where he also called Zillow's predicted values "wildly inaccurate and inconsistent."[16]

(In a rebuttal piece in the *Post*, Zillow's chief economist notes that it's nearly impossible for anyone to predict a home's sale price with 100 percent certainty, while conceding that real estate agents outperformed Zillow in a D.C.-area study. "Is a well-informed human better at pricing an individual home than a computer?" he asked. "The answer is yes, of course. But it's closer than you might think."[17])

So how should you interpret all of this information?

As you start to dig into the data, you'll see that Zillow provides something it calls a median error rate for each geographic area. The median error rate is a percentage, and it tells you that half of the Zestimates in that area will be closer to the final sale price than the error rate, and half will be further.

For example, when we looked at the data for Los Angeles, the median error rate was 7 percent. This means half of the homes sold for a price within 7 percent of their Zestimate (keep in mind it could be up to 7 percent lower *or* higher—so on a $800,000 house that's $744,000 to $856,000). Of course, the median error rate also means that half the homes sold for an amount *outside* this range—either *less* than 7 percent of the Zestimate, or *more* than 7 percent.[18]

(In some cases Zillow also gives what it calls a "Value Range," which shows the estimated high and low values for a home. This range, as it explains on its website, is in fact a 70 percent *confidence interval*, meaning that the home value should be within that range in 70 percent of an infinite number of samples.)

In other words, a Zestimate should be considered in the context of its median error rate. To its credit, Zillow displays the median error rate and explains what it is. It even simplifies everything with a four-star rating system that tells you how accurate the Zestimate is (as you might expect, the stars seem to correspond to the median error rate).[19]

The issue is that many people simply focus on the Zestimate without putting it in context, just as many people looking at poll don't consider the margin of error—they just look at who is "winning." But by ignoring the additional data—whether it's a median error rate, margin of error, or confidence interval—you're missing the big picture. Let's say you live in Washington, D.C., which had the highest Zestimate accuracy when we looked at Zillow's top metro areas.[20] If you're trying to sell a home with a Zestimate of $500,000, even if your house is within the median error rate of 5.0 percent (and remember, only half of the homes are), that means it could be $25,000 (5.0 percent of $500,000) more *or* less than the estimate. That's a $50,000 range.

Zestimates are also interesting because some people use them as a *forecast*, trying to determine what a house will sell for in the future. But Zillow clearly notes on its website that the Zestimate is based on what the home is worth "today."[21] Given that Zestimates are typically updated three times a week, it's quite possible that home sales in your area (or other factors) could change a home's Zestimate between the time you review it and the time your home sells. There are two lessons here—first of all, figure out if the data you're seeing is truly a prediction or not before you use it as such. And secondly, make sure that prediction error is accounted for, whether it's already added in, or you're adjusting for it.

Finally, consider what the Zestimate is based on. It's a proprietary formula, which means you don't know all the factors that go into it. It relies at least in part on *self-reported data*, which we know (in some cases) may not be 100 percent reliable. And the amount of data available may change from region to region, or even from week to week within the same region. When you don't have data, you need to work with the *sample* that you have. If there are more transactions in a certain area, that gives Zillow more data, and the Zestimates presumably become more accurate.

Or, as we think they should say—Zaccurate.

How to Be a Sound Consumer of Data

As always, we end the chapter with a list of five things you can do right now to be a better consumer of data. And since this is the last chapter in the book, let's take a look at the big picture. Here are five takeaways we hope you'll keep in mind as you encounter everydata in your everyday life.

1. **Recognize data** when you see and hear it. A newspaper article is data. A radio story is data. An e-mail newsletter from a vendor is data. Your kid's report card is data. Next week's sales forecast is data. A map is data. Wherever you live, whatever you do, you're likely surrounded by data each and every day.

2. **Get your facts right**. Many data issues are simply the result of a mistake. Perhaps there's a wrong formula in a spreadsheet or a misplaced decimal point in a key value. Maybe a blogger is unintentionally misrepresenting a new scientific study. One of the very first steps you should take is to verify that the data you're seeing is, in fact, accurate.

3. **Understand where the data is coming from**, and who is presenting it. In some cases, the person or organization may have an agenda, which means they may tailor the data (or cherry-pick it, if you will) to fit their message. After all, you don't typically hear the Democratic presidential candidate praising Republican-led initiatives (or vice versa). Even in cases where there is no obvious agenda, the data you consume typically comes from somewhere, is collected somehow, and is distributed by someone—all factors that can influence what ultimately ends up in front of you.

4. **Watch out for the obvious data traps**. There's a good chance you can open your hometown paper (or go to its website) and find a story that implies causation, when the only *proven* relationship in the data is a correlation. What are some other issues you're fairly likely to encounter on a regular basis, in our experience? Small sample sizes, findings that aren't statistically significant (or are statistically significant but have a very small effect), deceptive averages, and misleading visuals, including infographics.

5. **Understand that interpreting the data correctly will help you make better decisions**. Ultimately, this is what it comes down to— analyzing the data to get answers to questions that matter to you. How much higher will your company's sales be next quarter? Is the newest study about cancer-causing foods something you should worry about? What is the right price to pay for that summer home? Find the questions that will have the biggest impact on your life, and see how you can use the tools in this book to answer them.

THE END

This is the end.

Except it's not.

Because when you wake up tomorrow morning, you will be bombarded with more data. More examples of sampling and cherry picking.

More people confusing correlation for causation. More websites and blogs and newscasts, telling you what you should (and shouldn't) do to live longer, get smarter, and be better.

Hopefully, with everything you've learned in this book, you'll be able to see the misinformation hidden in all the "little data" you consume each day—and know exactly what to do with it.

GLOSSARY

Note that these are general definitions of some common terms. For more detail and context, please see the appropriate section of the text, as referenced in the index.

Aggregated data—Individual data points combined together into groups (e.g., the total number of votes in a state are aggregated to determine who receives that state's Electoral College votes)

Average—A type of summary statistic (usually the mean, mode, or median) that describes the data in a single metric

Big data—Data that's too big for people to process without the use of sophisticated machinery or computing capacity, given its enormous volume

Bivariate relationship—A fancy way of saying that there is a relationship between two ("bi") variables ("variate") (e.g., the price of your house is related to the number of bathrooms it has)

Black swan event—Something that is highly improbable, yet has a massive impact when it occurs

Causation—A relationship where it is determined that one factor causes another factor

Cherry-picking—Choosing anecdotal examples from the data to make your point, while ignoring other data points that may contradict it

Confidence interval—A way to measure the level of statistical certainty about results; typically expressed as a range of values, the confidence interval tells you the range of values within which you're likely to see the estimate (assuming, of course, you have a random—and representative—sample)

Confidence level—The term we use to determine how confident we are that we're measuring the data correctly

Confirmation bias—The tendency to interpret data in a way that reinforces your preconceptions

Correlation—A type of statistical relationship between two variables, usually defined as positive (moving in the same direction) or negative (moving in opposite directions)

Data—Information or facts

Dependence—When one variable is said to be directly determined by another

Deterministic forecast—A forecast for which you determine a precise outcome (e.g., it will rain tomorrow at 9 a.m. at my house)

Economic impact—How much something is going to cost in terms of time, money, health, or other resources

Estimate—A statistic capturing an inference about a population from a sample of data

Everydata—The term we use to describe everyday data

External validity—The extent to which the results from your sample can be extended to draw meaningful conclusions about the full population

False positive—A situation in which the statistical forecast predicts an untrue outcome (e.g., your credit card company calls you suspecting a recent purchase you actually made was fraudulent)

Forecast—A statement about the future; while forecast and prediction may have different meanings to specific groups of people (see chapter 8), we generally use them synonymously unless noted otherwise

Forecast bias—The term used to describe when a prediction is consistently high (a positive forecast bias) or low (a negative bias)

Inference—The process of making statistical conclusions about the data

Magnitude—Essentially, the size of the effect

Margin of error—A way to measure statistical uncertainty

Mean—What most people think of when you say "average" (to get the mean, you add up all the values, then divide by the number of data points)

Median—The middle value in a data set that has been rank ordered

Misrepresentation—When data is portrayed in an inaccurate or misleading manner

Mode—The data point (or points) most frequently found in your data

Observation—Looking at one unit, such as a person, a price, or a day

Odds—In statistics, the odds of something happening is the ratio of the probability of an outcome to the probability that it doesn't occur (e.g., a horse's statistical odds of winning a race might be ⅓, which means it is probable that the horse will win one out of every three races; in betting jargon, the odds are typically the reverse, so this same horse would have 2–1 odds against, which means it has a ⅔ chance of losing)

Omitted variable—A variable that plays a role in a relationship, but may be overlooked or otherwise not included; omitted variables are one of the primary reasons why correlation doesn't equal causation

Outlier—A particular observation that doesn't fit; it may be much higher (or lower) than all the other data, or perhaps it just doesn't fall into the pattern of everything else that you're seeing

P-hacking—Named after p-values, p-hacking is a term for the practice of repeatedly analyzing data, trying to find ways to make nonsignificant results significant

P-value—A way to measure statistical significance; the lower your p-value is, the less likely it is that the results you're seeing are due to chance

Population—The entire set of data or observations that you want to study and draw inferences about; statisticians rarely have the ability to look at the entire population in a study, although it could be possible with a small, well-defined group (e.g., the voting habits of all 100 U.S. senators)

Prediction—See *forecast*

Prediction error—A way to measure uncertainty in the future, essentially by comparing the predicted results to the actual outcomes, once they occur

Prediction interval—The range in which we expect to see the next data point

Probabilistic forecast—A forecast where you determine the probability of an outcome (e.g., there is a 30 percent chance of thunderstorms tomorrow)

Probability—The likelihood (typically expressed as a percentage, fraction, or decimal) that an outcome will occur

Proxy—A factor that you believe is closely related (but not identical) to another difficult-to-measure factor (e.g., IQ is a proxy for innate ability)

Random—When an observed pattern is due to chance, rather than some observable process or event

Risk—A term that can mean different things to different people; in general, risk takes into account not only the probability of an event, but also the consequences

Sample—Part of the full population (e.g., the set of *Challenger* launches with O-ring failures)

Sample selection—A potential statistical problem that arises when the way a sample has been chosen is directly related to the outcomes one is studying; also, sometimes used to describe the process of determining a sample from a population

Sampling error—The uncertainty of not knowing if a sample represents the true value in the population or not

Selection bias—A potential concern when a sample is comprised of those who chose to participate, a factor which may bias the results

Spurious correlation—A statistical relationship between two factors that has no practical or economic meaning, or one that is driven by an omitted variable (e.g., the relationship between murder rates and ice cream consumption)

Statistic—A numeric measure that describes an aspect of the data (e.g., a mean, a median, a mode)

Statistical impact—Having a statistically significant effect of some undetermined size

Statistical significance—A probability-based method to determine whether an observed effect is truly present in the data, or just due to random chance

Summary statistic—Metric that provides information about one or more aspects of the data; averages and aggregated data are two examples of summary statistics

Weighted average—An average calculated by assigning each value a weight (based on the value's relative importance)

NOTES

Preface

1. "Osamu Corporation Voluntarily Recalls Frozen Yellow Fin Tuna Chunk Meat Due to Possible Health Risk," U.S. Food and Drug Administration Recall Press Release, July 21, 2015, http://www.fda.gov/Safety/Recalls/ucm455622. htm; "Barber Foods Recalls Stuffed Chicken Products Due to Possible Salmonella Enteritidis Contamination," United States Department of Agriculture News Release, July 12, 2015, http://www.fsis.usda.gov/wps/portal/fsis/topics/recalls-and-public-health-alerts/recall-case-archive/archive/2015/recall-096-2015-release; "Aspen Foods Recalls Frozen, Raw, Stuffed & Breaded Chicken Products Due to Possible Salmonella Enteritidis Contamination," United States Department of Agriculture News Release, July 15, 2015, http://www.fsis.usda.gov/wps/portal/fsis/topics/recalls-and-public-health-alerts/recall-case-archive/archive/2015/recall-101-2015-release.

2. Jenna Birch, "Why Recent Food Poisoning Outbreaks All Began in This One State," Yahoo! Health, July 24, 2015, https://www.yahoo.com/health/why-do-so-many-foodborne-illness-outbreaks-begin-124925339332.html. According to the article, Minnesota is better than other states because it is "incredibly thorough and quick" in terms of interviewing people who may be involved in cases, and because it does additional DNA analysis to identify the source of the illness. In other words, Minnesota is using data to solve the problem.

3. No confidential or client information has been used in the preparation of this book. This book represents only the views of the authors, not other economists or employees of Edgeworth Economics.

Chapter 1

1. Roger E. Bohn and James E. Short, "How Much Information? 2009 Report on American Consumers" (San Diego, University of California: Global Information Industry Center, December 2009), 1–36, http://hmi.ucsd.edu/pdf/HMI_2009_ConsumerReport_Dec9_2009.pdf.

2. The BBC cited a professor who estimated one GB as the equivalent of a pickup truck filled with printed pages. "Britons Growing 'Digitally Obese,'" BBC News website, December 9, 2004, http://news.bbc.co.uk/2/hi/technology/4079417.stm.

3. That said, as the UC San Diego study explains, some of this data consumption happens simultaneously. For example, you might have the radio on as you work on your laptop.

4. Arthur D. Santana, Randall Livingstone, and Yoon Cho, "Medium Matters: Newsreaders' Recall and Engagement with Online and Print Newspapers," Print in the Mix website, accessed August 22, 2015, http://printinthemix.com/Research/Show/90.

5. As the organization that operates the Express Lanes explains it, "Sensors alongside the road monitor traffic levels and speed, and toll prices adjust to maintain free-flowing conditions in the Lanes—even during peak times—to provide value to customers." "Using the Express Lanes," Express Lanes website, accessed September 1, 2015, https://www.expresslanes.com/faqs.

6. Lev Grossman, "The Old Answer to Humanity's Newest Problem: Data," Time website, June 25, 2015, http://time.com/3935273/how-art-solves-the-data-problem/?iid=toc_062515.

7. On its website, IBM defines big data as "data sets whose size or type is beyond the ability of traditional relational databases to capture, manage, and process the data with low-latency." "What Is Big Data Analytics?," IBM website, accessed August 22, 2015, http://www-01.ibm.com/software/data/infosphere/hadoop/what-is-big-data-analytics.html.

8. Mary Schlangenstein, "UPS Crunches Data to Make Routes More Efficient, Save Gas," Bloomberg Business, October 30, 2013, http://www.bloomberg.com/news/articles/2013-10-30/ups-uses-big-data-to-make-routes-more-efficient-save-gas.

9. Toby Wolpe, "Big Data Deluge: How Dutch Water Is Trying to Turn the Tide," ZDnet website, October 1, 2013, http://www.zdnet.com/article/big-data-deluge-how-dutch-water-is-trying-to-turn-the-tide/.

10. Alice Truong, "How Naturebox Uses Big Data to Stock Your Snack Pantry," Fast Company website, June 4, 2014, http://www.fastcompany.com/3031078/fast-feed/how-naturebox-uses-big-data-to-stock-your-snack-pantry.

11. "IBM Research Breakthrough Helps Public Health Officials Improve Food Safety," IBM website, July 3, 2014, accessed July 29, 2015, https://www-03.ibm.com/press/us/en/pressrelease/44295.wss.

12. Louis Columbus, "Where Big Data Jobs Will Be in 2015," Forbes website, December 29, 2014, http://www.forbes.com/sites/louiscolumbus/2014/12/29/where-big-data-jobs-will-be-in-2015/.

13. Lindsay Gellman, "Big Data Gets Master Treatment at B-Schools," Wall Street Journal website, November 5, 2014, http://www.wsj.com/articles/big-data-gets-master-treatment-at-b-schools-1415226291.

14. Joe Keohane, "How Facts Backfire," Boston.com website, July 11, 2010, http://www.boston.com/bostonglobe/ideas/articles/2010/07/11/how_facts_backfire/.

15. *Data Analysis Report Fire and Emergency Medical Services Hermosa Beach, California* (Washington, D.C.: ICMA Center for Public Safety Management, August 2013), 1–52, http://www.hermosabch.org/modules/showdocument.aspx?documentid=3314.

16. Seth Godin, "Compared to What: Marketing and Relativity," *Seth Godin Blog*, September 23, 2013, http://sethgodin.typepad.com/seths_blog/2013/09/marketing-and-relativity.html.

17. Katherine Rosman, "Weather Channel Now Also Forecasts What You'll Buy," *Wall Street Journal* website, August 14, 2013, http://www.wsj.com/articles/SB10001424127887323639704579012674092402660.

18. Sy Syms was born Seymore Merinsky, but his family changed their name to Merns when Sy's dad and brother opened a store with the same name. Sy opened a competing store, but when he lost a legal fight to call it "Sy Merns," he renamed it SYMS—and then changed his own name to match. "Sy Syms, Founder of SYMS Corp., Dies at Age 83," *PR Newswire* website, November 17, 2009, accessed July 29, 2015, http://www.prnewswire.com/news-releases/sy-syms-founder-of-syms-corp-dies-at-age-83-70407382.html.

Chapter 2

1. Ronald Reagan, "*Challenger* Memorial Speech," January 31, 1986, Johnson Space Center, Houston, Texas, YouTube, accessed April 25, 2015, https://www.youtube.com/watch?v=PhI9OQp6ADg.

2. President Reagan used this phrase—originally penned by British aviator John Gillespie Magee—in a speech to the nation on the day of the accident, at 5 p.m. EST on January 28, 1986, YouTube, https://www.youtube.com/watch?v=qoQlkFryriQ.

3. Andrew J. Dunar and Stephen P. Waring, *Power to Explore—History of Marshall Space Flight Center 1960–1990* (Washington, D.C.: National Aeronautics and Space Administration, NASA History Office, Office of Policy and Plans, 1990), 339.

4. Report of the Presidential Commission on the Space Shuttle *Challenger* Accident (aka the Rogers Commission Report) (1986), chapter IV.

5. Rogers Commission Report, chapter IV.

6. According to the Rogers Commission Report, chapter IV, the temperature near the joint that failed was estimated to be 28 degrees Fahrenheit, +/- 5 degrees. The temperature on the opposite side of the booster—which faced the sun—was estimated to be 50 degrees Fahrenheit.

7. There were at least three potential issues with low temperatures. The first is O-ring resiliency. The second, as explained by the Rogers Commission Report

(chapter IV), was "the potential for ice in the joints." Finally, as the report noted, "O-ring hardness is also a function of temperature and may have been another factor in joint performance."

8. Kevin Smokler, "The Day That Gen X Grew Up," *Baltimore Sun*, February 3, 2006.

9. According to the Rogers Commission, "the Thiokol Management reversed its position and recommended the launch of 51-L, at the urging of Marshall and contrary to the views of its engineers in order to accommodate a major customer" (Rogers Commission Report, chapter V).

10. Bob Lund, quoted in the Rogers Commission Report, chapter V.

11. Various tests were actually conducted as low as 30 degrees. However, these experiments were conducted on test devices, and did not always include the putty that was part of the sealing system.

12. You should also note that, while Figure 2-1 displays the number of incidents, it does not accurately convey the *amount* of thermal distress. According to the Rogers Commission Report, the worst "blow-by" (a symptom of distress) occurred at 53 degrees. Looking at this chart, you can only see how many incidents there were—not how serious each one was.

13. Ann E. Tenbrunsel and Max H. Bazerman, "Launching Into Unethical Behavior: Lessons from the *Challenger* Disaster," *Freakonomics* blog, June 1, 2011, accessed April 25, 2015, http://freakonomics.com/2011/06/01/launching-into -unethical-behavior-lessons-from-the-challenger-disaster/.

14. To be fair, looking at the sample incorrectly was just one of the issues cited by the Rogers Commission Report, which also cited "a faulty design unacceptably sensitive to a number of factors" (chapter IV). The putty used to help seal gaps was also the subject of much debate, given that NASA changed suppliers (the original contractor used asbestos, and later stopped making the putty). Leak checks—meant to ensure the integrity of the putty and O-ring seal—also had the unfortunate effect of creating "dangerous gaps in the putty," according to *Power to Explore*. Many articles and books have explored the various reasons for the tragedy, and it is certainly not our intention to state (or even imply) that the sampling error alone caused the disaster. We only use it to illustrate our point. Communication (or lack thereof) was also a key component. In one particularly damning section of chapter V of the Rogers Commission Report, the commission noted that the decision makers "were unaware of the recent history of problems concerning the O-rings and the joint and were unaware of the initial written recommendation of the contractor advising against the launch at temperatures below 53 degrees Fahrenheit and the continuing opposition of the engineers at Thiokol after the management reversed its position . . . If the decisionmakers had known all of the facts, it is highly unlikely that they would have decided to launch 51-L [the name for the flight] on January 28, 1986."

15. "Frequently Asked Questions About the Space Shuttle and International Space Station," Kennedy Space Center website, accessed April 25, 2015, http://www .nasa.gov/centers/kennedy/about/information/shuttle_faq.html#1.

16. There are many issues with sampling—these are only two of them. We explore a few more concerns—including sampling error—in chapter 5. That said, this book is meant to be educational and entertaining, and shouldn't be taken as a comprehensive treatise on every issue that can arise with sampling (or any other topic).

17. Joseph Henrich, Steven J. Heine, and Ara Norenzayan, "The Weirdest People in the World?," *Behavioral and Brain Sciences* 33 (2010): 61.

18. Jeffrey J. Arnett, "The Neglected 95%: Why American Psychology Needs to Become Less American," *American Psychologist* 63, no. 7 (October 2008): 602.

19. Arnett, "Neglected 95%," 602.

20. Henrich et al., "Weirdest People," 6.

21. Henrich et al., "Weirdest People," 19.

22. John M. Grohol, "Psychology Secrets: Most Psychology Studies Are College Student Biased," *PsychCentral* blog, last reviewed August 26, 2010, accessed April 25, 2015, http://psychcentral.com/blog/archives/2010/08/26/psychology -secrets-most-psychology-studies-are-college-student-biased/.

23. Arnett, "Neglected 95%," 604.

24. Grohol, "Psychology Secrets."

25. Henrich et. al., "Weirdest People," 3.

26. "Research Findings," NWCR, accessed March 31, 2015, http://nwcr.ws/ Research/published%20research.htm.

27. "NWCR Facts," NWCR, accessed March 31, 2015, http://nwcr.ws/Research/ default.htm.

28. Deborah Netburn, "High Chair Injuries up 22% in 7 Years; How to Keep Your Baby Safe," *Los Angeles Times*, December 9, 2013.

29. "There Is Something Remarkable Happening Here," Nationwide Children's website, accessed April 25, 2015, http://www.nationwidechildrens.org/hospital -overview.

30. The data was only from some hospitals. According to its website ("National Electronic Injury Surveillance System (NEISS)," United States Consumer Product Safety Commission website, accessed April 25, 2015, http://www.cpsc.gov/ en/Research--Statistics/NEISS-Injury-Data/), NEISS offers "a national probability sample of hospitals in the U.S. and its territories" for injuries related to consumer products. The total number of injuries is then estimated, based on this sample of approximately 100 hospitals (the sample size changed throughout the years). Is that a large enough sample size? Is it a representative sample? While we have no reason to believe that the sampling was misguided (and we'd need another chapter to fully explore it), we do want to point out that this is yet

another instance in which sampling has the potential to significantly impact the everydata in our lives.

31. Check out SaferCar.gov. Just keep in mind that some rankings are relative to all other vehicles—while some results "can only be compared to other vehicles in the same class and whose weight is plus or minus 250 pounds of the vehicle being rated," http://www.safercar.gov/Vehicle+Shoppers/5-Star+FAQ#one. In other words, a three-star-rated SUV could theoretically be safer than a five-star compact car.

32. Rachel M. Kurinsky, Lynne M. Rochette, and Gary A. Smith, "Pediatric Injuries Associated with High Chairs and Chairs in the United States, 2003–2010," *Clinical Pediatrics* 53, no. 4 (2014).

33. "Syracuse Named Top Party School," Syracuse University website, accessed July 20, 2015, http://www.syracuse.com/news/index.ssf/2014/08/syracuse_named_top_party_school_princeton_review.html.

34. "Syracuse University," *U.S. News and World Report* website, accessed March 16, 2015, http://colleges.usnews.rankingsandreviews.com/best-colleges/syracuse-university-2882.

35. Rob Hoskin, "The Dangers of Self-Report," British Science Association Brainwaves website, March 3, 2012, accessed September 1, 2015, http://www.sciencebrainwaves.com/the-dangers-of-self-report/.

36. Allan F. Williams, "Views of U.S. Drivers About Driving Safety," *Journal of Safety Research* 34, no. 5 (2003): 491–494, doi:10.1016/j.jsr.2003.05.002.

37. S. Connor Gorber, M. Tremblay, D. Moher, and B. Gorber, "A Comparison of Direct vs. Self-Report Measures for Assessing Height, Weight and Body Mass Index: A Systematic Review," *Obesity Reviews* 8, no. 4 (July 2007): 307–326, http://www.ncbi.nlm.nih.gov/pubmed/17578381.

38. Each state gets a certain number of votes in the Electoral College, based in part on the number of seats it has in the U.S. House of Representatives. These seats are allocated based on the results of the U.S. Census. For example, after the 2010 census, 8 states gained members and 10 states had fewer members.

39. "Decennial Census of Population and Housing," United States Census Bureau website, accessed March 9, 2015, https://www.census.gov/programs-surveys/decennial-census/about.html.

40. "What Is the 1990 Undercount?," United States Census Bureau website, accessed March 9, 2015, https://www.census.gov/dmd/www/techdoc1.html.

41. Amy Sullivan, "Why the 2010 Census Stirs Up Partisan Politics," *Time* magazine, February 15, 2009. On a related note, to make up for the people who aren't counted (or are counted more than once), the U.S. Census Bureau conducts a post-enumeration survey. This survey samples households, then compares that data with the original census data. The Census Bureau uses this sample data to

develop adjusted population counts. But not everybody wants an adjustment—especially if it's going to increase the number of people who might vote against you in the next election. As the *Time* magazine article noted, "In very general terms, Republicans would prefer to err on the side of undercounting and Democrats would prefer to err on the side of overcounting."

42. *Congressional Record*, H1602, March 24, 1999, http://www.gpo.gov/fdsys/pkg/CREC-1999-03-24/pdf/CREC-1999-03-24-pt1-PgH1602.pdf.

43. "Is Gluten-free Eating a Trend Worth Noting?," NPD Group website, accessed April 25, 2015, https://www.npd.com/perspectives/food-for-thought/gluten-free-2012.html.

44. Kathie Rowell, "Growing Number of People Choosing Gluten-free Lifestyle," *Shreveport Times*, April 13, 2015.

45. "Celiac Disease: Fast Facts," National Foundation for Celiac Awareness website, accessed April 25, 2015, http://www.celiaccentral.org/celiac-disease/facts-and-figures/.

46. David Katz, "Is Gluten-Free Just a Fad?," *Huffington Post* website, last updated September 24, 2011, accessed April 25, 2015, http://www.huffingtonpost.com/david-katz-md/gluten-free-diet_b_907027.html.

47. "School Data," Chicago Public Schools website, accessed April 25, 2015, http://cps.edu/SchoolData/Pages/SchoolData.aspx.

48. "NWEA Measures of Academic Progress (MAP)," Chicago Public Schools website, accessed April 25, 2015, http://cps.edu/SchoolData/Documents/NWEA_MAPFactSheet.pdf.

49. We downloaded the spreadsheet on March 8, 2015, at http://cps.edu/SchoolData/Pages/SchoolData.aspx.

50. Troy A. LaRaviere, "Drop CPS' Reform Strategy: CPS Neighborhood School Growth Outpaces Charters," *Chicago Sun Times*, September 1, 2014.

51. And we're certainly not going to get on a soapbox to talk about the pros and cons of charters versus public schools or the wisdom of standardized testing. Although if you want to learn more, a guest post on the *Brain Pickings* blog is an interesting read: Anya Kamenetz, "5 Reasons Standardized Testing Won't Slow Down," *Penelope Trunk* blog, last reviewed March 5, 2015, http://education.penelopetrunk.com/2015/03/05/5-reasons-standardized-testing-wont-slow-down/.

52. Art Golab, Becky Schlikerman, and Lauren FitzPatrick, "CPS Outpaces Charter Schools in Improvements, Especially in Reading," *Chicago Sun Times*, October 1, 2014.

53. Barack Obama, "The Raid That Killed Bin Laden," *60 Minutes*, May 9, 2011. http://www.cbsnews.com/news/president-obama-on-the-raid-that-killed-bin-laden/.

54. As quoted in *Ratings Analysis: Theory and Practice* by James Webster, Patricia Phalen, and Lawrence Lichty, (Lawrence Erlbaum Associates, 1991), 113.

Chapter 3

1. "Take the Money and Run," Steve Miller Band, from the album *Fly Like an Eagle* (Capitol, 1976).
2. *Election Summary Report,* November 14, 2012, http://assets01.aws.connect .clarityelections.com/Assets/Connect/RootPublish/elpaso-tx.connect.clarity elections.com/ElectionResults/2012_ElectionDocs/110612/ELECTION _RESULTS_ED.pdf, accessed through El Paso County Elections website (https://www.epcountyvotes.com/).
3. See, for example, "Are Red or Blue States Better Job Creators?," CNBC, accessed August 16, 2015, http://www.cnbc.com/2015/08/13/are-red-or-blue-states-better-job-creators.html; "Climate Battle Will Likely Divide Red States and Blue States Down a Green Line," *National Journal,* accessed August 15, 2016, http:// www.nationaljournal.com/next-america/newsdesk/climate-epa-regulation-obama-states-20150803; Steve Benen, "'Obamacare' Thrives in Nation's Largest Blue State," the *Maddow Blog,* accessed August 16, 2015, http://www.msnbc .com/rachel-maddow-show/obamacare-thrives-nations-largest-blue-state.
4. All maps are from http://www-personal.umich.edu/~mejn/election/2012/. Mark Newman, "Maps of the 2012 US Presidential Election Results," from the personal page associated with the University of Michigan website, updated November 8, 2012, http://www-personal.umich.edu/~mejn/election/2012/. Text and images used under Creative Commons license: http://creativecommons .org/licenses/by/2.0/.
5. You also see a lot of red, which is surprising given that Obama won, until you realize that the illustration is a map based on the size of the state rather than its population. On Newman's website ("Maps of 2012"), he offers cartograms that provide a different look at the results. And in case you were wondering, the two states that do not follow a strict winner-take-all approach are Maine and Nebraska, which can split their votes among multiple candidates.
6. Newman, "Maps of 2012."
7. Federal Election Commission, Federal Elections 2012: *Election Results for the U.S. President, the U.S. Senate and the U.S. House of Representatives* (Washington D.C., July 2013), http://www.fec.gov/pubrec/fe2012/federalelections2012.pdf.
8. John F. Helliwell, Richard Layard, and Jeffrey Sachs (eds.), *World Happiness Report 2015* (New York: Sustainable Development Solutions Network, 2015), http://worldhappiness.report/.
9. The data comes from the Gallup World Poll, which asks people to evaluate their lives on a scale of 0 to 10 using a tool known as the Cantril Self-Anchoring Striving Scale. The scale is named for Hadley Cantril, a researcher who studied, among other things, people's reaction to Orson Welles's famous *War of the Worlds* radio broadcast. The Cantril scale asks people to think of their life

satisfaction as a ladder, and rank their life as the best (10) or worst (0) or somewhere in between. Hadley Cantril, *The Pattern of Human Concerns* (New Brunswick, NJ: Rutgers University Press, 1966).

10. *Personal Well-Being Across the UK, 2012/13.* Contains public sector information licensed under the Open Government Licence v3.0. Permitted under license. "Open Government Licence for Public Sector Information," the National Archives website, accessed July 9, 2015, http://www.nationalarchives.gov.uk/doc/open-government-licence/version/3/.

11. Thanks to Richard Strausz, a board member of the Detroit Area Council of Teachers of Mathematics—and Mike's wife's uncle—for the inspiration for this section.

12. "Chelsea Apartments," Yateswood.com, accessed August 5, 2015, http://www.yateswood.com/sites/default/files/property-files/Chelsea%20Offering_0.pdf.

13. Julia La Roche, "Here's How Much 10 of the Richest People in the World Made per Minute in 2013," *Business Insider,* December 19, 2013, http://www.businessinsider.com/what-warren-buffett-makes-per-hour-2013-12#ixzz3jyUhYnBx.

14. "March of Dimes Peristats," March of Dimes website, accessed July 10, 2015, http://www.marchofdimes.org/peristats/ViewTopic.aspx?dv=mt&reg=12086&top=2&lev=0&slev=6; "2014 Greater Miami Jewish Federation Population Study: A Portrait of the Miami Jewish Community," Greater Miami Jewish Federation website, accessed July 10, 1015, http://jewishmiami.org/population study/ and Census Bureau data.

15. Raymond Britt, "Boston Marathon 2015 Statistical Analysis," Competitor.com, updated April 22, 2015, http://running.competitor.com/2015/04/photos/boston-marathon-2015-statistical-analysis_127026.

16. Julie Adams, "Who Weighs the Aussie Average?," Marie Claire.com.au website, accessed July 10, 2015, http://nicolepartridge.com/wp-content/uploads/2012/05/MC05_FEAT_70kg.pdf.

17. "Simply Salary: Mayor," Simply Hired website, accessed July 10, 2015, http://www.simplyhired.com/salaries-k-mayor-jobs.html; "Simply Salary: Deputy Mayor," Simply Hired website, accessed July 10, 2015, http://www.simplyhired.com/salaries-k-deputy-mayor-jobs.html. And yes, we have some concerns about the accuracy of this data for numerous reasons, including that it's only from online job listings, and that the source doesn't define *average* (we're assuming it's mean, but can't be sure). That said, we've chosen to include this example because it illustrates a much-needed point about how sample sets can impact averages.

18. "How Much Mayors Make, Langley Council Plans Review of Mayor's Salary," *South Whidbey Record,* May 22, 2011, http://www.southwhidbeyrecord.com/news/122414919.html.

19. "Mayor, Office of the (OTM)," NYC Citywide Administrative Services website, accessed July 3, 2015, http://a856-gbol.nyc.gov/gbolwebsite/390.html. In fact,

the first deputy mayor (who is second in command) has a higher salary than the mayor—although this could be because the mayor receives other benefits, including the use of Gracie Mansion on the city's Upper East Side.

20. As one of John's colleagues noted, this could be seen primarily as a selection issue. His point was that a more accurately selected sample would not be misleading, because we could either look at just a sample that had mayors *and* deputy mayors, or we could look at all cities and put in a zero as the deputy mayor's salary for cities that don't have a deputy mayor. Either way, you would likely get an answer showing that the deputy, on average, makes less than the mayor.

21. Cameron Keng, "Employees Who Stay in Companies Longer Than Two Years Get Paid 50 Percent Less," *Forbes* website, June 22, 2014, http://www.forbes.com/sites/cameronkeng/2014/06/22/employees-that-stay-in-companies-longer-than-2-years-get-paid-50-less/.

22. Bob Papper, *Research: RTDNA Salary Survey,* Radio Television Digital News Association website, July 13, 2015, http://www.rtdna.org/article/research_rtdna_salary_survey#.VaUV00XFTbU.

23. "UK Politics, How Poll Tracker Works," BBC News website, April 10, 2015, http://www.bbc.com/news/uk-politics-13248622; Real Clear Politics, http://www.realclearpolitics.com/.

24. Sam Wang, "On the Track Record of Simple Poll Aggregation," Princeton Election Consortium website, October 24, 2008, http://election.princeton.edu/2008/10/24/on-the-track-record-of-simple-poll-aggregation/.

25. For example, some statisticians and economists look for three or four standard deviations (which is a statistical measure of how spread out the data is) as an indicator of an outlier.

26. John W. Emerson and Silas Meredith, *Nationalistic Judging Bias in the 2000 Olympic Diving Competition,* August 22, 2010, http://www.stat.yale.edu/~jay/EmersonMaterials/MathHorizons.pdf. The specific event in which the outcome may have changed was women's 10-meter platform, which the authors explored in: John W. Emerson, Miki Seltzer, and David Lin, "Assessing Judging Bias: An Example from the 2000 Olympic Games," *American Statistician* 63, no. 2 (2009): 124–131.

27. Emerson and Meredith, *Nationalistic Judging.*

28. Robert W. Hayden, "A Dataset That Is 44 Percent Outliers," *Journal of Statistics Education* 13, no. 1 (2005), www.amstat.org/publications/jse/v13n1/datasets.hayden.html.

29. An exception being if every value in the data set is identical.

30. Conwood Company was purchased by Reynolds American, Inc., and changed its name to American Snuff Company, LLC, effective January 1, 2010.

31. You can read more about the case here: Benjamin Klein and Joshua D. Wright, "Antitrust Analysis of Category Management: *Conwood v. United States*

Tobacco," November 10, 2006, http://www.justice.gov/sites/default/files/atr
/legacy/2006/12/01/219951.pdf.

32. Herbert Hovenkamp, *The Antitrust Enterprise: Principle and Execution* (Cambridge, MA: Harvard University Press, 2008), 81.

33. Hovenkamp, *The Antitrust Enterprise,* 81.

34. *American Time Use Survey,* Bureau of Labor Statistics website, last modified September 30, 2014, http://www.bls.gov/tus/charts/sleep.htm.

35. Christopher Ingraham, "The Average American Woman Now Weighs As Much As the Average 1960s Man," *Washington Post Wonkblog,* June 12, 2015, http://www.washingtonpost.com/news/wonkblog/wp/2015/06/12/look-at-how-much-weight-weve-gained-since-the-1960s/.

36. "By the Numbers: What Americans Drink in a Year," *Huffington Post* website, June 27, 2011, http://www.huffingtonpost.com/2011/06/27/americans-soda-beer_n_885340.html.

37. Nicholas Carlson, "If You Drive Fewer Than 9,480 Miles per Year, It's Cheaper to Take an Uber Everywhere Than to Own a Car," *Business Insider* website, September 17, 2014, http://www.businessinsider.com/is-uber-cheaper-than-owning-a-car-2014-9.

38. Grace Gold, "Do Americans Shower More or Less Than the Rest of the World?," Yahoo! Health website, February 20, 2015, https://www.yahoo.com/health/do-americans-shower-more-or-less-than-the-rest-of-111508762932.html.

39. *Employee Tenure in 2014,* Bureau of Labor Statistics website, September 18, 2014, http://www.bls.gov/news.release/tenure.nr0.htm.

40. Paul Ausick, "Most Americans Are Smarter Than the Average American," *24/7 Wall Street* website, May 18, 2014, http://247wallst.com/economy/2014/05/18/most-americans-are-smarter-than-the-average-american/.

41. Melissa Dahl, "Most of Us Think We're Hotter Than Average, Survey Says," NBC News website, September 8, 2010, http://www.nbcnews.com/id/39044399/ns/health-skin_and_beauty/t/most-us-think-were-hotter-average-survey-says/#.VcO_OflViko.

42. Ola Svenson, "Are We All Less Risky and More Skillful Than Our Fellow Drivers?," *Acta Psychologica* 47, no. 2 (February 1981): 143–148.

43. "Podcast," *A Prairie Home Companion* website, accessed September 1, 2015, http://prairiehome.org/listen/podcast/.

44. If you want to learn more about these biases, pick up a copy of Daniel Kahneman's *Thinking, Fast and Slow* (New York: Farrar, Straus and Giroux, 2013).

45. Adrian Furnham, Joanna Moutafi, and Thomas Chamorro-Premuzic, "Personality and Intelligence: Gender, the Big Five, Self-Estimated and Psychometric Intelligence," *International Journal of Selection and Assessment* 13 (March 4, 2005): 11–24, doi: 10.1111/j.0965-075X.2005.00296.x.

46. Okay, so this isn't a perfect comparison. A rotten apple literally spoils the bunch by emitting ethylene, a gas that makes the fruit around it ripen more. An outlier

doesn't typically change the data around it—it simply affects the conclusions that you draw from that data. But even though the mechanisms differ, the point is the same—one apple/outlier can change the results.

Chapter 4

1. GSV EDU, *Education Sector Factbook 2012,* accessed April 21, 2015, http://gsvadvisors.com/wordpress/wp-content/uploads/2012/04/GSV-EDU-Factbook-Apr-13-2012.pdf.
2. "People Who Wear Glasses Are Smarter, Study Claims," AOL website, July 1, 2014, http://www.aol.com/article/2014/07/01/people-who-wear-glasses-are-smarter-study-claims/20923473/.
3. David Goldman, "Smarter People Use iPhones—Study," CNN Money website, January 22, 2015, http://money.cnn.com/2015/01/22/technology/mobile/iphone-smart-study/.
4. "What the Public Knows About the Political Parties," Pew Research Center website, April 11, 2012, http://www.people-press.org/2012/04/11/what-the-public-knows-about-the-political-parties/.
5. Marisa Taylor, "Books and Music That Make You Dumb," *Wall Street Journal* website, February 27, 2009, http://blogs.wsj.com/digits/2009/02/27/books-and-music-that-make-you-dumb/.
6. Ned Hepburn, "Smarter People Stay Up Later, Do More Drugs and Have More Sex—It's Science," *Esquire* website, November 21, 2013, http://www.esquire.com/news-politics/news/a26244/smart-means-sex-and-drugs-and-staying-up/.
7. Maria Konnikova, "Sinister Minds: Are Left-Handed People Smarter?" *New Yorker* website, August 22, 2013, http://www.newyorker.com/tech/elements/sinister-minds-are-left-handed-people-smarter.
8. Satoshi Kanazawa, "Why Intelligent People Drink More Alcohol," *Psychology Today* website, posted on October 10, 2010, in the Scientific Fundamentalist, https://www.psychologytoday.com/blog/the-scientific-fundamentalist/201010/why-intelligent-people-drink-more-alcohol.
9. "Infographic: iPhone Usage Rates by State," Chitika, Inc. website, January 22, 2015, https://chitika.com/insights/2015/iphone-by-state.
10. Assuming the sampling was done correctly, which we would probably question given that they only sampled people during one week of the year—which also happened to be the week of Christmas.
11. "People Who Wear Glasses," AOL.
12. Satoshi Kanazawa and Kaja Perina, "Why Night Owls Are More Intelligent," *Personality and Individual Differences* 47 (2009): 685–690, https://personal.lse.ac.uk/kanazawa/pdfs/paid2009.pdf.

13. Kim Bhasin, "If Your Commute Lasts More Than 45 Minutes, You Will Probably Get Divorced," *Business Insider* website, June 2, 2011, http://www.business insider.com/long-commutes-can-cause-divorce2011-6 accessed 4/21/15.

14. Lauren Martin, "Sleep Naked, Dream Bigger: Why the Secret to a Better Life Is As Simple As Taking It Off," *Elite Daily* website, August 18, 2014, http://elite daily.com/life/gotta-free-sleep-free-people-sleep-naked-happier/715351/.

15. Morgan Gibson, "Living Near a Starbucks Will Increase Your Home's Value," *People's* "Great Ideas" website, January 29, 2015, http://greatideas.people .com/2015/01/29/starbucks-increases-home-value/?xid=socialflow_twitter _peoplemag.

16. Spencer Rascoff and Stan Humphries, "Confirmed: Starbucks Knows the Next Hot Neighborhood Before Everybody Else Does," *Quartz* website, January 28, 2015, http://qz.com/334269/what-starbucks-has-done-to-american-home-values/.

17. Rascoff and Humphries, "Confirmed."

18. John Moore, "Starbucks Real Estate Learnings," *Brand Autopsy* blog, May 19, 2005, http://www.brandautopsy.com/2005/05/starbucks_real_.html; Rubinfeld's book is *Built for Growth: Expanding Your Business Around the Corner or Across the Globe* (FT Press, 2005).

19. Emma Brown, "How Does a Teacher's Race Affect Which Students Get to Be Identified As 'Gifted?'" *Washington Post* website, April 22, 2015, http:// www.washingtonpost.com/news/local/wp/2015/04/22/how-does-a-teachers -race-affect-which-students-get-to-be-identified-as-gifted/.

20. Emily Oster, "Take Back Your Pregnancy," *Wall Street Journal* website, August 9, 2013, http://www.wsj.com/news/articles/SB1000142412788732351440457865 2091268307904.

21. "The Value of Google Result Positioning," Chitika website, June 7, 2013, https://chitika.com/google-positioning-value.

22. "Algorithms," Google website, accessed April 20, 2015, http://www.google .com/insidesearch/howsearchworks/algorithms.html. Here, you'll also find a link to "The Anatomy of a Large-Scale Hypertextual Web Search Engine," in which Sergey Brin and Larry Page presented Google.

23. "Search Engine Ranking Factors 2015," Moz website, accessed September 1, 2015, https://moz.com/search-ranking-factors/correlations.

24. "Search Engine Ranking Factors 2015, Expert Survey and Correlation Data," Moz website, accessed September 1, 2015, https://moz.com/search-ranking-factors/ correlations.

25. Rand Fishkin, "What Do Correlation Metrics Really Tell Us About Search Rankings?," *Rand Fishkin Blog,* Moz website, January 14, 2013, http://moz .com/rand/what-do-correlation-metrics-really-tell-us-about-search-rankings/.

26. Kate Bratskeir, "Grilled Cheese Lovers Have More Sex and Are Better People, According to Survey," *Huffington Post* website, April 8, 2015, http://www.huffingtonpost.com/2015/04/08/grilled-cheese-sex-bow-chica-bow-wow_n_7027572.html.

27. The "Cheddar Makes It Better" commercials from America's Dairy Farmers National Dairy Board were some of our favorites back in the day. You can see one here: https://www.youtube.com/watch?v=ypx8-7bzLX8.

28. Tyler Vigen, "Spurious Correlations—Sunlight in California Correlates with Lawyers in American Samoa," Tyler Vigen website, accessed April 20, 2015, http://tylervigen.com/view_correlation?id=30444.

29. Tyler Vigen, "Spurious Correlations—Total Revenue Generated by Bowling Alleys (US) Correlates with Per Capita Consumption of Sour Cream (US)," Tyler Vigen website, accessed April 20, 2015, http://tylervigen.com/view_correlation?id=292.

30. Tyler Vigen, *Spurious Correlations* (New York: Hachette Books, 2015).

31. "Infographic: iPhone Usage Rates by State," Chitika Inc., January 2015, https://chitika.com/insights/2015/iphone-by-state.

32. "Infographic: iPhone Usage Rates by State," Chitika Inc., January 2015, https://chitika.com/files/iPhone_Usage_by_State-Correlation_White_Paper_Chitika Insights.pdf#overlay-context=user/5.

33. For an alternative view exploring the potential psychological influence of such lucky routines, see "Why 'Magical Thinking' Works for Some People" by Piercarlo Valdesolo in *Scientific American* (October 19, 2010), http://www.scientificamerican.com/article/superstitions-can-make-you/.

34. Transcripts—CNN *Larry King Live*, "Jenny McCarthy's Austism Fight," CNN website, aired April 2, 2008, http://transcripts.cnn.com/TRANSCRIPTS/0804/02/lkl.01.html. This is the same interview in which McCarthy says, "I believe that parents' anecdotal information is science-based information."

35. "Survey: One Third of American Parents Mistakenly Link Vaccines to Autism," National Consumers League website, April 2, 2014, http://www.nclnet.org/survey_one_third_of_american_parents_mistakenly_link_vaccines_to_autism.

36. A. J. Wakefield, S. H. Murch, A. Anthony, J. Linnell, D. M. Casson, M. Malik, M. Berelowitz, A. P. Dhillon, M. A. Thomson, P. Harvey, A. Valentine, S. E. Davies, and J. A. Walker-Smith, "Ileal-Lymphoid-Nodular Hyperplasia, Non-Specific Colitis, and Pervasive Developmental Disorder in Children," Lancet 375, no. 9713 (2010) http://www.thelancet.com/journals/lancet/article/PIIS0140-6736%2897%2911096-0/abstract. Retracted due to the fact that the investigations were not approved by the local ethics committee and that children were not "consecutively referred."

37. Anjali Jain, Jaclyn Marshall, Ami Buikema, Tim Bancroft, Jonathan P. Kelly, and Craig J. Newschaffer, "Autism Occurrence by MMR Vaccine Status Among

US Children with Older Siblings with and without Autism," *JAMA* 313, no. 15 (2015), http://jama.jamanetwork.com/article.aspx?articleid=2275444. Although, if you want to start poking holes, you could start with the fact that the sample set was "privately insured children with older siblings."

Chapter 5

1. Randomization is a powerful statistical tool for eliminating selection bias, and Esther Duflo and others have written extensively about randomized controlled trials and related topics. For more detail, "Using Randomization in Development Economics Research: A Toolkit," © 2006 by Esther Duflo, Rachel Glennerster, and Michael Kremer, National Bureau of Economic Research, 2006, http://www.nber.org/papers/t0333.pdf.
2. February 29 was included in the dates to account for men born in leap years.
3. David E. Rosenbaum, "Statisticians Charge Draft Lottery Was Not Random," *New York Times,* January 4, 1970, http://frewm.wikispaces.com/file/view /nytimes.pdf. If you look at the original article, you'll see that the average number for July was reported as 180. Based on our calculations, it was actually 182.
4. Rosenbaum, "Statisticians Charge Draft Lottery Was Not Random."
5. Stephen E. Fienberg, "Randomization and Social Affairs: The 1970 Draft Lottery," *Science* 171 (1971): 255, http://conallboyle.com/lottery/05USmil_ draft1970.pdf.
6. We might also be able to learn something about the process by studying the variance—the amount by which values vary—within each month.
7. John McCormick, "Donald Trump Dominates Republican Field in Pre-Debate Bloomberg Poll," Bloomberg, August 4, 2015, http://www.bloomberg.com/ politics/articles/2015-08-04/donald-trump-dominates-republican-field-in-pre -debate-bloomberg-poll.
8. With a margin of error of ±4.4 percent, the researchers would expect that Jeb would not be more than 4.4 percent higher or lower than 10 percent (approximately 6 to 14 percent), and that Walker would not be more than 4.4 percent higher or lower than 8 percent (roughly 4 to 12 percent).
9. "Bloomberg Politics National Poll," Bloomberg, August 4, 2015, http://images .businessweek.com/cms/2015-08-04/8302475320_tue.pdf.
10. Of course, there may be other factors that affect sampling error—such as whether you're polling all voters versus likely voters, how you're conducting the poll (some pollsters may only call land lines, not cell phones), etc.
11. Les Picker, "Media Bias and Voting," National Bureau of Economic Research, http://www.nber.org/digest/oct06/w12169.html.
12. "Secondhand Smoke and Cancer," NIH National Cancer Institute website, reviewed January 12, 2011, http://www.cancer.gov/about-cancer/causes-prevention/risk/ tobacco/second-hand-smoke-fact-sheet#r5.

13. "About This Website," NIH National Cancer Institute website, posted April 10, 2015, http://www.cancer.gov/about-website.

14. This number appears to be an estimate from an EPA report: "Approximately 3,000 lung cancer deaths per year among nonsmokers (never-smokers and former smokers) of both sexes are estimated to be attributable to ETS in the United States. While there are statistical and modeling uncertainties in this estimate, and the true number may be higher or lower, the assumptions used in this analysis would tend to underestimate the actual population risk. The overall confidence in this estimate is medium to high." U.S. EPA, "Respiratory Health Effects of Passive Smoking (Also Known As Exposure to Secondhand Smoke or Environmental Tobacco Smoke, ETS?)," U.S. Environmental Protection Agency, Office of Research and Development, Office of Health and Environmental Assessment, Washington, D.C., EPA/600/6-90/006F, 1992.

15. Judy Peres, "No Clear Link Between Passive Smoking and Lung Cancer," *Journal of the National Cancer Institute* 105 (2013): 1844–1846, http://jnci.oxford journals.org/content/early/2013/12/05/jnci.djt365.full.

16. *Thank You for Smoking*, Fox Searchlight Pictures website, accessed August 9, 2015, http://www.foxsearchlight.com/thankyouforsmoking/.

17. Ultimately, a statistical analysis is trying to determine if there is enough evidence to reject a null hypothesis. As Jesse Farmer wrote on the *20bits* blog, "Don't read anything into the fact that it's called the 'null' hypothesis—it's just the hypothesis we're trying to test." (Jesse Farmer, "Hypothesis Testing: The Basics," *20bits* blog, April 22, 2009, http://20bits.com/article/hypothesis-testing-the-basics). Typically, a null hypothesis is usually one where there is no relationship between two variables. In other words, your data can't tell you one way or the other whether or not there is a relationship—it could simply be due to random chance. When you reject the null hypothesis, it means that there is an association that is likely not due to chance.

18. That said, even Fisher appears to have had some flexibility on the .05, saying. "If one in twenty does not seem high enough odds, we may, if we prefer it, draw the line at one in fifty (the 2 per cent point), or one in a hundred (the 1 per cent point)." Ronald A. Fisher, "The Arrangement of Field Experiments," *Journal of the Ministry of Agriculture of Great Britain* 33 (1926): 503–513, accessed August 9, 2015, https://digital.library.adelaide.edu.au/dspace/bit stream/2440/15191/1/48.pdf.

19. Regina Nuzzo, "Scientific Method: Statistical Errors," *Nature* website, February 12, 2014, http://www.nature.com/news/scientific-method-statistical-errors -1.14700.

20. As Daniels noted, this approach is not what hypothesis testing is all about. In our opinion, it's also important to keep in mind that "statistically significant," as many people understand it ($p<.05$), does not mean the findings are 100 percent

certain. The p-value measures probability, which means that some results may still be more probable than others. For example, p-values of .001 and .049 are both statistically significant (by this definition), but a lower p-value means that these results are more likely to be true. (To be technically precise, it actually means that finding a lack of a relationship between two variables is more likely to be false.)

21. They did find one group of women—those who lived with a smoker for at least 30 years—that did show a higher risk for lung cancer, but even that finding was, according to the researchers, "of only borderline statistical significance."

22. Matthew Hankins, "Still Not Significant," *Probable Error* blog, April 21, 2013, https://mchankins.wordpress.com/2013/04/21/still-not-significant-2/.

23. Alison Jing Xu, Norbert Schwarz, and Robert S. Wyer, Jr., "Hunger Promotes Acquisition of Nonfood Objects," *Proceedings of the National Academy of Sciences* 112, no. 9 (March 3, 2015), http://www.pnas.org/content/112/9/2688.abstract; read the *New Yorker* overview here: Nicola Twilley, "The Good, the Bad, and the Hangry," *New Yorker* website, March 10, 2015, http://www.newyorker.com/tech/elements/hunger-good-bad-hangry.

24. Allison Aubrey, "Even if You're Lean, 1 Soda Per Day Ups Your Risk of Type 2 Diabetes," NPR website, July 23, 2015, http://www.npr.org/sections/thesalt/2015/07/23/425635400/even-if-youre-lean-1-soda-per-day-ups-your-risk-of-diabetes.

25. Fumiaki Imamura, Laura O'Connor, Zheng Ye, Jaako Mursu, Yasuaki Hayashino, Shilpa N. Bhupathiraju, and Nita G. Forouhi, "Consumption of Sugar Sweetened Beverages, Artifically Sweetened Beverages, and Fruit Juice and Incidence of Type 2 Diabetes: Systematic Review, Meta-Analysis, and Estimation of Population Attributable Fraction," *BMJ* 351(2015), doi: http://dx.doi.org/10.1136/bmj.h3576.

26. On February 12, 2002, Rumsfeld (former U.S. secretary of defense) appeared at a U.S. Department of Defense briefing and said: "There are known knowns; there are things we know we know. We also know there are known unknowns; that is to say, we know there are some things we do not know. But there are also unknown unknowns—the ones we don't know we don't know." On Rumsfeld's website (http://papers.rumsfeld.com/about/page/authors-note), he says he "first heard a variant of the phrase 'known unknowns' in a discussion with former NASA administrator William R. Graham, when we served together on the Ballistic Missile Threat Commission in the late 1990s."

27. John P. A. Ioannidis, "Why Most Published Research Findings Are False," *Public Library of Science Medicine* 2, no. 8 (August 30, 2005): doi:10.1371/journal.pmed.0020124.

28. Tom Siegfried, "Odds Are, It's Wrong," *ScienceNews* 177, no. 7 (March 27, 2010): 26, https://www.sciencenews.org/article/odds-are-its-wrong.

29. Honor Whiteman, "Study Links Coffee Intake with Reduced Risk of Endometrial Cancer," *Medical News Today* website, February 6, 2015, accessed August 13, 2015, http://www.medicalnewstoday.com/articles/288988.php.
30. Whiteman, "Study Links Coffee Intake."
31. We thank Susan Dynarski for pointing this example out to us.
32. Joshua A. Krisch, "We Give Up. Let's Just Say Coffee Cures Everything," Vocativ website, January 26, 2015, http://www.vocativ.com/culture/health-culture/coffee-cures-cancer/.
33. Jonathan D. Schoenfeld and John P. A. Ioannidis, "Is Everything We Eat Associated with Cancer? A Systematic Cookbook Review," *American Journal of Clinical Nutrition* 97 no. 1 (2013): 127–134, doi: 10.3945/ajcn.112.047142.
34. Emily Oster, "You Don't Need 8 Glasses of Water a Day," *FiveThirtyEight Science* website, posted September 30, 2014, http://fivethirtyeight.com/features/you-dont-need-8-glasses-of-water-a-day/.
35. Kathleen Doheny, "Coffee May Lower Endometrial Cancer Risk," WebMD website, February 6, 2015, http://www.webmd.com/cancer/news/20150206/coffee-linked-to-possible-lower-endometrial-cancer-risk.
36. Megan L. Head, Luke Holman, Rob Lanfear, Andrew T. Kahn, and Michael D. Jennions, "The Extent and Consequences of P-Hacking in Science," *Public Library of Science (PLoS) Biology* 13, no. 3 (2015): e1002106, doi: 10.1371/journal.pbio.1002106.
37. Jonah Lehrer, "The Truth Wears Off," *New Yorker* website, December 13, 2010, http://www.newyorker.com/magazine/2010/12/13/the-truth-wears-off.
38. Rebecca Steinbach, Chloe Perkins, Lisa Tompson, Shane Johnson, Ben Armstrong, Judith Green, Chris Grundy, Paul Wilkinson, and Phil Edwards, "The Effect of Reduced Street Lighting on Road Casualties and Crime in England and Wales: Controlled Interrupted Time Series Analysis," *Journal of Epidemiology Community Health* (June 3, 2015), doi: 10.1 136/jech-2015-206012, http://jech.bmj.com/content/early/2015/07/08/jech-2015-206012.full.pdf+html.
39. Michael Reilly, "Shark Attacks: What Are the Odds?" *Discovery News* website, August 2, 2010, http://news.discovery.com/animals/sharks/shark-attacks-what-are-the-odds-20100802.htm.
40. *Sharknado 3,* Syfy website, accessed August 20, 2015, http://www.syfy.com/sharknado3.
41. Bill Gates, "The Deadliest Animal in the World," April 25, 2014, Gatesnotes website, http://www.gatesnotes.com/Health/Most-Lethal-Animal-Mosquito-Week.

Chapter 6

1. Here's a very basic explanation of how it works: picture a globe inside a cylinder. Now, project each point on the globe straight out until it makes a mark on the cylinder. Unroll the cylinder, and you have a Mercator map.

2. Another issue with the Mercator map is that, because it skews the size of objects so much at the poles, it's not uncommon for part of Antarctica to be cropped out. This has the effect of truncating the Southern Hemisphere, and therefore making the Northern Hemisphere appear larger in comparison.

3. And you're welcome to read all about them here: Melita Kennedy, "Understanding Map Projections," Environmental Systems Research Institute Inc., 2000, http://kartoweb.itc.nl/geometrics/map%20projections/understanding%20map%20projections.pdf.

4. Full disclosure: Mike's wife is a teacher. Yes, she has tenure. No, she's not in California.

5. Beatriz Vergara v. State of California and California Teachers Association, Dept. 58, No. BC484642 (August 27, 2014), http://studentsmatter.org/wp-content/uploads/2014/08/SM_Final-Judgment_08.28.14.pdf.

6. Jordan Weissmann, "Fuzzy Math," *Slate* website, accessed July 18, 2015, http://www.slate.com/articles/business/moneybox/2014/06/judge_strikes_down_california_s_teacher_tenure_laws_a_made_up_statistic.html.

7. "David Berliner," Arizona State website, accessed July 18, 2015, http://berliner.faculty.asu.edu/wordpress/. Oh, and in case you were wondering, the Sun Devil logo was designed by a former Walt Disney employee, and (according to some) supposedly resembles Mr. Disney in a not-so-flattering way. "Sun Devil Athletics," the Sun Devils website, accessed July 18, 2015, http://www.thesundevils.com/ViewArticle.dbml?ATCLID=208256866&DB_OEM_ID=30300; Paul Lukas, "The Disney/ESPN Connection Suddenly Makes a Lot More Sense," Uni Watch website, December 18, 2012, http://www.uni-watch.com/2012/12/18/how-walt-disney-designed-the-umkc-mascot-character/.

8. See Appleseednetwork.org for details.

9. There were other issues with how Berliner's testimony ended up as a key point in the judge's decision. For example, Berliner claimed that he never used the words "grossly ineffective." And his testimony (based on the *Slate* article) doesn't seem to directly link bad teachers to low test scores.

10. Hannah Arem, Steven C. Moore, Alpa Patel, Patricia Hartge, Amy Berrington de Gonzalez, Kala Visvanathan, Peter T. Campbell, Michal Freedman, Elisabete Welderpass, Hans Olov Adami, Martha S. Linet, L-Min Lee, and Charles E. Mathews, "Leisure Time Physical Activity and Mortality," *JAMA Internal Medicine*, published online April 6, 2015, doi:10.1001/jamainternmed.2015.0533.

11. Nathan Yau, "Fox News Makes the Best Pie Chart. Ever," *Flowing Data* website, accessed August 4, 2015. http://flowingdata.com/2009/11/26/fox-news-makes-the-best-pie-chart-ever/. The pie chart was aired on Fox Chicago, and the source was given as Opinion Dynamics.

12. David Yanofsky, "The Chart Tim Cook Doesn't Want You to See," *Quartz* website, September 10, 2013, http://qz.com/122921/the-chart-tim-cook-doesnt -want-you-to-see/.

13. For a stunning look at how data can be captured, check out www.dear -data.com—"a year-long, analog data drawing project" by two extremely talented information designers: Giorgia Lupi and Stefanie Posavec, "Dear Data," accessed June 7, 2015, http://www.dear-data.com/.

14. "American Time Use," Bureau of Labor Statistics website, http://data.bls .gov/cgi-bin/surveymost?tu.

15. For a discussion of what type of visualization to use, check out our blog post on the topic at http://www.johnhjohnsonphd.com/blog2/blog/2015/4/18 /a-guide-to-data-visualization.

16. "To Make Your Claim More Believable, Simply Add a Graph," *Harvard Business Review,* https://hbr.org/2014/10/to-make-your-claim-more-believable-simply -add-a-graph. The original research is here: Aner Tal and Brian Wansink, "Blinded with Science: Trivial Graphs and Formulas Increase Ad Persuasiveness and Belief in Product Efficacy," *Public Understanding of Science,* October 15, 2014, doi: 10.1177/0963662514549688.

17. "Menu Engineering: How to Raise Restaurant Profits 15% or More," Menu Cover Depot website, accessed June 16, 2015, http://www.menucoverdepot .com/resource-center/articles/restaurant-menu-engineering/.

18. John Burn-Murdoch, "Why You Should Never Trust Data Visualisation," *Guardian* website, July 24, 2013, http://www.theguardian.com/news/ datablog/2013/jul/24/why-you-should-never-trust-a-data-visualisation.

19. "PETA's Beauty Without Bunnies Program, Companies That Do Test on Animals," PETA, accessed June 7, 2015, http://www.mediapeta.com/peta/PDF/ companiesdotest.pdf.

20. *Last Week Tonight with John Oliver*, Episode 3: "Climate Change Debate," *Last Week Tonight* video, 4:27, HBO, May 11, 2014, http://www.hbo.com/last-week-tonight-with-john-oliver/episodes/01/03-may-11-2014/video/climate-change-debate.html?autoplay=true.

21. Bryan Beverly, "3 Old Tricks for the Analytics Hall of Shame," All Analytics website, November 25, 2013, http://www.allanalytics.com/author.asp?section _id=1828&doc_id=269454&f_src=allanalytics_sitedefault&utm_source=dlvr .it&utm_medium=twitter.

22. A quick response (QR) code is a type of bar code that users can scan using their smartphones to get video and other content.

23. Bob Hoffman, "How Marketers Lie to Themselves," *Ad Contrarian* blog, April 20, 2015, http://adcontrarian.blogspot.com/2015/04/how-marketers-lie-to-themselves. html.

24. John Stossel, "Running on Empty," ABC News website, June 5, 2008, http://abcnews.go.com/2020/Stossel/story?id=3989000.

25. Lauren Brennan, Mando Watson, Robert Klaber, Tagore Charles, "The Importance of Knowing Context of Hospital Episode Statistics When Reconfiguring the NHS," *BMJ* 2012; 344:e2432.

26. Kimberly Warner, Walker Timme, Beth Lowell, and Michael Hirshfield, "Oceana Study Reveals Seafood Fraud Nationwide," Oceana website, February 2013, http://oceana.org/sites/default/files/reports/National_Seafood_Fraud_Testing_Results_FINAL.pdf.

27. *"Guidance for Industry: A Food Labeling Guide* (9. Appendix A: Definitions of Nutrient Content Claims)," U.S. Food and Drug Administration website, January 2013, http://www.fda.gov/Food/GuidanceRegulation/GuidanceDocumentsRegulatory-Information/LabelingNutrition/ucm064911.htm.

28. Peter Coy, "FAQ: Reinhart, Rogoff, and the Excel Error That Changed History," *Bloomberg Business* website, April 18, 2013, http://www.bloomberg.com/bw/articles/2013-04-18/faq-reinhart-rogoff-and-the-excel-error-that-changed-history.

29. "*Wikipedia*: About," *Wikipedia*, accessed June 13, 2015, https://en.wikipedia.org/wiki/Wikipedia:About.

30. That said, even when the data does come from a trusted media source, you should at least recognize the fact that a few large media conglomerates are responsible for much of the news and entertainment you consume on a daily basis, which could have a significant effect on what you see and hear.

31. "Ten Things You May Not Know About *Wikipedia*," *Wikipedia*, accessed June 13, 2015, https://en.wikipedia.org/wiki/Wikipedia:Ten_things_you_may_not_know_about_Wikipedia#You_can.27t_actually_change_anything_in_Wikipedia.E2.80.A6.

32. "Food Product Dating," United States Department of Agriculture website, accessed June 16, 2015, http://www.fsis.usda.gov/wps/portal/fsis/topics/food-safety-education/get-answers/food-safety-fact-sheets/food-labeling/food-product-dating/food-product-dating.

33. "Environmental Issues: Food and Agriculture, the Dating Game," Natural Resources Defense Council, accessed June 16, 2015, http://www.nrdc.org/food/expiration-dates.asp.

34. Read our full blog post on this topic—including some details on how much money wasted food might cost us—"Everydata of Expiration Dates," the *John H. Johnson, PhD Blog,* May 18, 2015, http://www.johnhjohnsonphd.com/blog2/blog/2015/4/18/expiring-soonbut-so-what.

35. The study included a "nationally representative sample of 5,000 adults between the ages of 16 and 65," with "similar nationally representative samples" from

other countries. On the numeracy test, "Compared with the U.S. average score, average scores in 18 countries were higher, in 2 countries they were lower, and in 2 countries they were not significantly different." So, while the U.S. was listed 21st out of 23, numbers 19 (Ireland) and 20 (France) were not "significantly" higher: Madeline Goodman, Robert Finnegan, Leyla Mohadjer, Tom Krenzke, and Jacquie Hogan, "Literacy, Numeracy, and Problem Solving in Technology Rich Environments Among U.S. Adults: Results from the Program for International Assessment of Adult Competencies 2012: First Look," U.S. Department of Education, National Center for Education Statistics, NCES 2014-008, October 2013, http://nces.ed.gov/pubs2014/2014008.pdf.

36. Elizabeth Green, "Why Do Americans Stink at Math?" *New York Times Magazine* website, July 23, 2014, http://www.nytimes.com/2014/07/27/magazine/why-do-americans-stink-at-math.html.

37. Kimihiko Yamagishi, "When a 12.86% Mortality Is More Dangerous Than 24.14%: Implications for Risk Communication," *Applied Cognitive Psychology* 11 (1997): 495–506.

38. Actually, we found two flat earth societies in a quick search, both of which are called the Flat Earth Society: http://www.theflatearthsociety.org/cms/; http://www.tfes.org/. Both accessed September 1, 2015.

39. Rebecca Burn-Callander, "Stupid Errors in Spreadsheets Could Lead to Britain's Next Corporate Disaster," *Telegraph* website, April 7, 2015, http://www.telegraph.co.uk/finance/newsbysector/banksandfinance/11518242/Stupid-errors-in-spreadsheets-could-lead-to-Britains-next-corporate-disaster.html.

Chapter 7

1. Even if you didn't want to pay attention, you still had to watch the commercial. DVRs and TiVo weren't readily available back then, and it was too much of a hassle to tape shows on your VHS player. And if you don't know what a VHS player is, go ask your parents.

2. Federal Trade Commission, *In the Matter of Gerber Products Company, Corporation*, Case and Proceedings Docket C-3744, last updated May 30, 1997, https://www.ftc.gov/sites/default/files/documents/cases/1997/05/c3744cmp.pdf.

3. "About the FTC," Federal Trade Commission website, accessed April 25, 2015, http://www.ftc.gov/about-ftc: "FTC Accuses Gerber of False and Misleading Advertising," Federal Trade Commission, March 12, 1997, https://www.ftc.gov/news-events/press-releases/1997/03/ftc-accuses-gerber-false-and-misleading-advertising.

4. Federal Trade Commission, "FTC Accuses Gerber."

5. Federal Trade Commission, "FTC Accuses Gerber."

6. Federal Trade Commission, "FTC Accuses Gerber."

7. Federal Trade Commission, *In the Matter of Gerber Products Company Corporation*, Agreement Containing Consent Order, File Number 962 3175,

accessed July 12, 2015, https://www.ftc.gov/sites/default/files/documents/cases/1997/03/gerber.pdf.

8. "What Does 'Cherry Picking' Mean?" Wisegeek website, accessed August 11, 2015, http://www.wisegeek.com/what-does-cherry-picking-mean.htm.

9. Edward J. Fox and Stephen J. Hoch, "Cherry-Picking," *Journal of Marketing* 69, no. 1 (2005): 46–62.

10. John Allen Paulos, "Why Do We Believe That Catastrophes Come in Threes?," ABC News website, July 5, 2009, http://abcnews.go.com/Technology/Whos Counting/story?id=7988416.

11. "2009: Deaths," *Wikipedia* website, accessed April 25, 2015, http://en.wikipedia.org/wiki/2009#Deaths. And no, we don't recommend *Wikipedia* as a primary source.

12. And, in case you're wondering, the three teams that *won* game one and went on to win the World Series were the '87 Twins, '84 Tigers, and the '80 Phillies. "1988 World Series-Game 1-Bottom of the 9th," Dailymotion website, accessed April 25, 2015, http://www.dailymotion.com/video/xd2fhk_1988 -world-series-game-1-bottom-of_sport.

13. It would not. While the team that lost game one went on to win the World Series 7 out of 10 years, that only happened in 3 out of the past 5 years, 11 out of the past 20 years, and 14 out of 30 (using 1988 as our reference year for all). That said, the broadcasters could have chosen an even more dramatic statistic by saying it happened 5 out of the past 7 years.

14. "The Escalator," *Skeptical Science* website, accessed September 2, 2015, http://www.skepticalscience.com/graphics.php?g=47.

15. "Willie Horton 1988 Attack Ad," YouTube, accessed April 25, 2015, http://www.youtube.com/watch?v=Io9KMSSEZ0Y.

16. Kenneth J. Cooper, "Bush Is Using Case of a Murderer to Assail Dukakis As Soft on Crime," Philly.com website, June 26, 1988, http://articles.philly .com/1988-06-26/news/26265230_1_michael-s-dukakis-furlough-program -massachusetts-gov.

17. *Fahrenheit 9/11*, directed by Michael Moore (Culver City, CA; Lions Gate Films, 2004.)

18. Brent Baker, "CBS Scolds Bush for Hiding How 'Kerry Talks Tough' on Terrorism," Media Reseach Center website, October 20, 2004, http://www.mrc.org/biasalerts/cbs-scolds-bush-hiding-how-kerry-talks-tough-terrorism-10202004.

19. Martin Kasindorf and Judy Keen, "'Fahrenheit 9/11': Will It Change Any Voter's Mind?" *USA Today* website, June 24, 2004, http://usatoday30.usatoday .com/news/politicselections/nation/president/2004-06-24-fahrenheit-cover_x.htm.

20. "Toothpastes," Colgate website, accessed July 12, 2015, http://www.colgate .com/en/us/oc/products/toothpaste.

21. Of course, cherry picking should not be confused with curating, which we typically think of as working on behalf of the audience, filtering the data to select

the most appealing/interesting data (as opposed to cherry pickers, who often deliberately select only some of the data in order to produce a specific result).

22. Andrew Simon, "Game 1 Rout Not Necessarily Precursor to Title," MLB.com website, October 23, 2013, http://m.mlb.com/news/article/63287950.

23. Burton G. Malkiel, "Returns from Investing in Equity Mutual Funds, 1971–1991," *Journal of Finance* 50 (1995), 549–572.

24. Not to mention the distinction between causation and correlation, which we talked about in chapter 4.

25. Esteemed economist Daniel Kahneman shared the Nobel Prize in 2002 for his work related to psychological factors that affect our decisions. Much of Kahneman's work was done in collaboration with Amos Tversky, who passed away in 1996 and was therefore ineligible for the Nobel Prize.

26. In case you're wondering, the first example is the Johns Hopkins Hospital ("The Johns Hopkins Hospital Ranked Among the Top Hospitals in the Nation in 2015," Johns Hopkins Medicine website, accessed September 1, 2015, http://www.hopkinsmedicine.org/usnews/); the second is Mayo Clinic (Mayo Clinic website homepage, accessed September 1, 2015, http://www.mayoclinic.org/); and the third is New York-Presbyterian ("Awards and Recognition," New York-Presbyterian website, accessed September 1, 2015, http://nyp.org/about/americas-top-doctors.html).

27. "Press Release: NCA Publishes Annual Consumption Tracking Study," National Coffee Association press release, June 18, 2013, http://www.ncausa.org/custom/headlines/headlinedetails.cfm?id=876&returnto=778. Retrieved 3/15/15.

28. Roberto Ferdman, "A Study About Butter, Funded by the Butter Industry, Found That Butter Is Bad for You," *Washington Post,* August 7, 2015, http://www.washingtonpost.com/news/wonkblog/wp/2015/08/07/the-butter-industry-probably-regrets-paying-for-this-study-that-shows-butter-is-bad-for-you/.

Chapter 8

1. Alan Buis, "Japan Quake May Have Shortened Earth Days, Moved Axis," NASA website, March 14, 2011, http://www.nasa.gov/topics/earth/features/japanquake/earth20110314.html.

2. The National Diet of Japan, "The Official Report of the Fukushima Nuclear Accident Independent Investigation Commission," 2012, https://www.nirs.org/fukushima/naiic_report.pdf.

3. Patrick J. Kiger, "Fukushima's Radioactive Water Leak: What You Should Know," August 9, 2013, *National Geographic News* website, http://news.nationalgeographic.com/news/energy/2013/08/130807-fukushima-radioactive-water-leak/.

4. International Atomic Energy Agency Mission Report, "The Great East Japan Earthquake Expert Mission, IAEA International Fact Finding Expert Mission of the Fukushima Dai-Ichi NPP Accident Following the Great East Japan

Earthquake and Tsunami," May 24, 2011, http://www-pub.iaea.org/MTCD/
meetings/PDFplus/2011/cn200/documentation/cn200_Final-Fukushima-
Mission_Report.pdf.

5. "J-SHIS Japan Seismic Hazard Information," J-SHIS Map website, accessed July
26, 2015, http://www.j-shis.bosai.go.jp/map/?lang=en. That said, the *Guardian*
noted that, "since 1979, every earthquake that caused 10 or more deaths has
struck in regions claimed to be at low risk." (Ian Sample and Justin McCurry,
"Flawed Earthquake Predicitions Gave Fukushima a False Sense of Security,"
Guardian website, April 13, 2011, http://www.theguardian.com/science/2011/
apr/13/flawed-earthquake-predictions-fukushima.)

6. *IAEA Mission Report.* Based on this data, the site level for key structures and systems was set at 4.0 meters, while the elevation for critical buildings was set at 10
meters. In 2002, Tokyo Electric Power Company (aka TEPCO, the plant operator) revised the estimated height of a tsunami to 5.7 meters. Then, on March 7,
2011—just four days before the deadly disaster—TEPCO told Japan's Nuclear
and Industrial Safety Agency that a future tsunami could be higher than 10
meters, according to an article in the *Asahi Shimbun* ("TEPCO Warned of Big
Tsunami 4 Days Prior to March 11," *Asahi Shimbun* website, August 25, 2011,
http://ajw.asahi.com/article/0311disaster/quake_tsunami/AJ201108257639).

7. Official Report, National Diet of Japan.

8. Official Report, National Diet of Japan.

9. IAEA Safety Standards Series, "Site Evaluation for Nuclear Installations, Safety
Requirements No. NS-R-3," International Atomic Energy Agency, November
2003, http://www-pub.iaea.org/MTCD/publications/PDF/Pub1177_web.pdf.

10. James M. Acton and Mark Hibbs, "Why Fukushima Was Preventable,"
Carnegie Endowment for International Peace, March 2012, http://carnegieen
dowment.org/files/fukushima.pdf.

11. Ludger Mohrbach et al., "Earthquake and Tsunami in Japan on March 11,
2011 and Consequences for Fukushima and Other Nuclear Power Plants," VGB
Power Tech (Germany), April 1, 2011, www.vgb.org/vgbmultimedia/News/
Fukushimav15VGB.pdf.

12. Martin Fackler, "Tsunami Warnings, Written in Stone," *New York Times,* April
20, 2011, http://www.nytimes.com/2011/04/21/world/asia/21stones.html
?_r=0.

13. Even the best model will not fully predict the past because there is, at least in
theory, truly random error. In fact, although it may seem counterintuitive, a
model that perfectly explains the past is often a sign of an "overfit" model and
will perform poorly in the future.

14. With complex forecasts—such as determining where a hurricane will make
landfall—forecasters may look at a set of models. Even small changes in the
model may have an impact on a forecast. For example, according to an article

on *IEEE Spectrum* (Tekla Perry, "Predicting Hurricane Sandy," accessed August 2, 2015, http://spectrum.ieee.org/tech-talk/computing/software/predicting -hurricane-sandy) simply using two different computers to run the same software may result in two different outcomes, since each computer may run calculations in a different order. But if the forecasters make minor changes and still find consistency in the various forecasts, they can rest (somewhat) assured that the models are accurate.

15. For example, building contracts frequently include what are called "force majeure" clauses that specify types of natural disasters that can result in delays in construction.

16. IAEA Mission Report.

17. "Earthquake Facts & Earthquake Fantasy," USGS website, accessed July 26, 2015, http://earthquake.usgs.gov/learn/topics/megaqk_facts_fantasy.php.

18. "Travelling with Your Visa Card," Visa website, accessed August 2, 2015, http://www.visa.ca/en/personal/travelling/index.jsp.

19. Of course, there are some situations that are entirely predictable. For example, if you have a fixed interest rate on a loan, you can calculate exactly what your payments will be for the future.

20. Statisticians may also measure the tolerance interval, which shows how confident we are that our prediction interval contains a certain percentage of the expected values.

21. "Howard Dean," YouTube video, 0:23, posted by Kittensaremegasilly, October 22, 2006, https://www.youtube.com/watch?v=KDwODbl3muE.

22. Daniel B. Murray and Scott W. Teare, "Probability of a Tossed Coin Landing on Edge," *Phys. Rev. E* 48, 2547 (October 1, 1993), http://journals.aps.org/pre/abstract/10.1103/PhysRevE.48.2547.

23. Andrew Gelman and Deborah Nolan, "You Can Load a Die, But You Can't Bias a Coin," *American Statistician* 56 (November 4, 2002), http://www.stat.columbia.edu/~gelman/research/published/diceRev2.pdf.

24. Erica Klarreich, "Toss Out the Toss-Up: Bias in Heads-or-Tails," *Science News Online*, 165, no. 9 (February 28, 2004): 131, http://web.archive.org/web/20080314023237/http://www.sciencenews.org/articles/20040228/fob2.asp.

25. Just make sure what you're looking at is truly an independent event. For example, if you're a basketball player shooting free throws, each throw is not an independent event. Yes, it's a separate event from the one before. But it's also influenced by other, past factors—everything from your fatigue to your state of mind after making (or missing) your past shot. That said, there is conflicting research in terms of whether or not athletes can have a so-called "hot hand," with one paper finding that "[t]he belief in the hot hand and the 'detection' of streaks in random sequences is attributed to a general misconception

of chance" (Thomas Gilovich, Robert Vallone, and Amos Tversky, "The Hot Hand in Basketball: On the Misperception of Random Sequences," *Cognitive Psychology* 17 (1985): 295–314, http://citeseerx.ist.psu.edu/viewdoc/summary?doi=10.1.1.115.6700), while a study from Harvard found that "players who are outperforming will continue to do so, conditional on the difficulty of their present shot" (Andrew Bocskocsky, John Ezekowitz, and Carolyn Stein, "The Hot Hand: A New Approach to an Old 'Fallacy,'" presented at the MIT Sloan Sports Analytics Conference, February 28–March 1, 2014, http://www.sloansportsconference.com/wp-content/uploads/2014/02/2014 _SSAC_The-Hot-Hand-A-New-Approach.pdf).

26. Ellen Davis, "Committing the 'Gambler's Fallacy' May Be in the Cards, New Research Shows," Texas A&M Health Science Center website, March 9, 2015, http://news.tamhsc.edu/?post=committing-the-gamblers-fallacy-may-be-in-the -cards-new-research-shows. Thanks to Ron Friedman for the find.

27. There's another way of looking at this, known as Bayesian probability (after the eighteenth-century English mathematician Thomas Bayes). With Bayesian probability, you use the data gathered to update your initial beliefs after the fact. It's the opposite of the way in which the gambler's fallacy works. As one of John's colleagues pointed out, it's the difference between knowing that a coin is fair and learning about the coin. So, a Bayesian might flip a coin 10 times, get heads all 10 times, and adjust his probability to say that the coin was always more likely to land heads up. Here's another way to think about it—consider a bowl full of M&M's on top of a shelf. You can reach inside the bowl, but not see inside it. Your initial belief is that approximately 24 percent of the M&M's are blue (the colors aren't equally distributed, according to a blog post from Josh Madison— https://joshmadison.com/2007/12/02/mms-color-distribution-analysis/—and other research). You reach inside, take out an M&M, observe the color (blue), and then put it back. You do this 10 times, and each time you get a blue M&M. For non-Bayesians, the probability of getting a blue M&M on your next turn is still 24 percent. But for a Bayesian, the probability is higher, since you've now revised your initial beliefs (based on the sample) to believe that more than 24 percent of the M&M's are blue.

28. "3 & 4 Digit, New York's Best Bi-Weekly Numbers Guide," Lotto Stats website, June 18, 2008, https://www.lotstats.com/pdf/lssampleissue.pdf. That said, if your goal is to split the jackpot with as few people as possible, there are strategies you can employ. For example, you can pick less popular numbers, such as those above 31 (since many people use dates as their "lucky" numbers), and you can choose consecutive strings of numbers, since many people think those combinations are less likely to win. Just don't forget about your favorite book authors when you hit it big.

29. "Performance," Employees Retirement System of Texas website, accessed July 23, 2015, http://www.ers.state.tx.us/About_ERS/Investments/Performance/.

30. "Women in Alternative Investments: Building Momentum in 2013 and Beyond," *Rothstein Kass Institute Second Annual Survey,* December 2012, https://nyhfr.org/documents/FG/hfrt/edu/70046_RK_WomeninAlternativeInvestmentsF.pdf.

31. Full disclosure: Mike's brother-in-law works for Eagle's View.

32. Kelly Brit, "Hedge Funds Trail Stocks for Fifth Year with 7.4% Return," *Bloomberg Business* website, January 8, 2014, http://www.bloomberg.com/news/articles/2014-01-08/hedge-funds-trail-stocks-for-fifth-year-with-7-4-return.

33. Rob Copeland and Gregory Zuckerman, "How Individual Investors Can Invest Like a Hedge Fund," *Wall Street Journal* website, August 3, 2014, http://www.wsj.com/articles/how-individual-investors-can-invest-like-a-hedge-fund-1407106285.

34. Stephanie Yang, "The Epic Story of How a 'Genius' Hedge Fund Almost Caused a Global Financial Meltdown," July 10, 2014, *Business Insider* website, http://www.businessinsider.com/the-fall-of-long-term-capital-management-2014-7#ixzz3kjpsJKfl.

35. Stephen Taub, "The 2015 Rich List: The Highest Earning Hedge Fund Managers of the Past Year," *Institutional Investor's Alpha* website, May 5, 2015, http://www.institutionalinvestorsalpha.com/Article/3450284/The-2015-Rich-List-The-Highest-Earning-Hedge-Fund-Managers-of-the-Past-Year.html.

36. Tim Jones, "Dewey Defeats Truman," *Chicago Tribune,* accessed July 16, 2015, http://www.chicagotribune.com/news/nationworld/politics/chi-chicagodays-deweydefeats-story-story.html. Perhaps you've seen the famous photo of Harry Truman holding up a copy of the paper, a photo taken two days after the election—a nearly unimaginable span of time in today's digital world. That said, the error was also due, in part, to a printers' strike, which meant that inexperienced typesetters were working at the paper on election night. In fact, on the same front page with the "Dewey Defeats Truman" headline, you can see five lines of upside-down type in the far-right column: Todd Andrlik, "Dewey Defeats Truman: The Rarely Told Story of *Chicago Tribune*'s Most Famous Issue," *Huffington Post* website, updated May 25, 2011, http://www.huffingtonpost.com/todd-andrlik/dewey-defeats-truman-the_b_119351.html.

37. Will Lester, "'Dewey Defeats Truman' Disaster Haunts Pollsters," *Los Angeles Times* website, November 1, 1998, http://articles.latimes.com/1998/nov/01/news/mn-38174.

38. Lester, "'Dewey Defeats Truman' Disaster."

39. Thurmond and Wallace each pulled in 2.4 percent of the popular vote nationwide, although—given the nature of the U.S. Electoral College system—

Thurmond carried four Southern states, while Wallace carried none. The 1948 race had all sorts of interesting twists and turns. Thurmond got one Electoral College vote from Tennessee, as faithless elector Preston Parks decided not to vote for Truman, who had carried the state. (Faithless electors—those who don't follow their party's wishes—are an example of a variable that can disrupt predictions.) In addition, due to efforts by Dixiecrats, Truman was left off the ballot in Alabama, despite the fact that he was the sitting president and the official Democratic Party nominee.

40. Ben Cosgrove, "Behind the Picture: 'Dewey Defeats Truman' and the Politics of Memory," *Time* website, May 4, 2014, http://time.com/3879744/dewey-defeats-truman-the-story-behind-a-classic-political-photo/.

41. Michael Lewis, "In Nature's Casino," *New York Times Magazine*, August 26, 2007, http://www.nytimes.com/2007/08/26/magazine/26neworleans-t.html?pagewanted=all&_r=0.

42. James Fallows, "When a 1-in-a-Billion Chance of Accident May Not Seem 'Safe Enough,'"*Atlantic* website, March 28, 2014, http://www.theatlantic.com/technology/archive/2014/03/when-a-1-in-a-billion-chance-of-accident-may-not-seem-safe-enough/359780/.

43. Carl Bialik, "Odds Are, Stunning Coincidences Can Be Expected," *Wall Street Journal* website, updated September 24, 2009, http://www.wsj.com/articles/SB125366023562432131, accessed August 2, 2015.

44. Taleb cites the rise of the Internet and the events of September 11, 2001, as examples of events with black swan characteristics in his book *The Black Swan: The Impact of the Highly Improbable,* 2nd ed., with a new section: "On Robustness and Fragility" (Incerto), Random House (2010).

45. Brad M. Barber and Terrance Odean, "Trading Is Hazardous to Your Wealth: The Common Stock Investment Performance of Individual Investors," *Journal of Finance* LV (April 2, 2000), http://citeseerx.ist.psu.edu/viewdoc/download?doi=10.1.1.139.1931&rep=rep1&type=pdf.

46. Harold Maass, "The Odds Are 11 Million to 1 That You'll Die in a Plane Crash," *The Week* website, July 8, 2013, http://theweek.com/articles/462449/odds-are-11-million-1-that-youll-die-plane-crash.

47. Marcus Buckingham, "Most HR Data Is Bad Data," *Harvard Business Review*, February 9, 2015, https://hbr.org/2015/02/most-hr-data-is-bad-data.

48. "The Seinfeld Chronicles: An Obsessive-Compulsive Dissection of All 169 Episodes," *Entertainment Weekly* website, May 4, 1998, http://www.ew.com/article/1998/05/04/seinfeld-chronicles.

Chapter 9

1. Joe Pinsker, "Why Do Former High-School Athletes Make More Money?," *Atlantic*, May 28, 2015, http://www.theatlantic.com/business/archive/2015/05

/why-do-former-high-school-athletes-make-more-money-and-get-better
-jobs/394283/.

2. Kevin M. Kniffin, Brian Wansink, and Mitsuru Shimizu, "Sports at Work. Anticipated and Persistent Correlates of Participation in High School Athletics," *Journal of Leadership & Organizational Studies* 22, no. 2 (May 2015): 217–230, doi: 10.1177/1548051814538099.

3. Aebra Coe, "How Much Money Does It Take to Make A Lawyer Happy?" *Law360* website, August 17, 2015, http://www.law360.com/articles/691712/how-much-money-does-it-take-to-make-a-lawyer-happy.

4. Andrew Strickler, "Nonequity Partners the Most Miserable Attys in Your Firm," *Law360* website, August 17, 2015, http://www.law360.com/articles/691856/nonequity-partners-the-most-miserable-attys-in-your-firm.

5. "ABA National Lawyer Population Survey. Historical Trend in Total National Lawyer Population 1878–2015," American Bar Association, accessed August 17, 2015, http://www.americanbar.org/content/dam/aba/administrative/market_research/total-national-lawyer-population-1878-2015.authcheckdam.pdf.

6. Jacob Batchelor, "Bigger Is Better When It Comes to Making Lawyers Happy," *Law360* website, August 17, 2015, http://www.law360.com/articles/691835/bigger-is-better-when-it-comes-to-making-lawyers-happy.

7. Ana Swanson, "Scientists Have Discovered How the Month You're Born Matters for Your Health," *Washington Post* website, June 15, 2015, http://www.washingtonpost.com/news/wonkblog/wp/2015/06/15/what-your-birth-month-means-for-your-risk-of-disease/.

8. Mary Regina Boland, Zachary Shahn, David Madigan, George Hripcsak, and Nicholas P. Tatonetti, "Birth Month Affects Lifetime Disease Risk: A Phenome-Wide Method," *Journal of the American Medical Informatics Association* (June 3, 2015), doi: http://dx.doi.org/10.1093/jamia/ocv046.

9. The reasons vary based on the medical condition. For example, the researchers (citing other studies) noted that "individuals born in seasons with more abundant home dust mites had a 40% increased risk of developing asthma complicated by dust mite allergies," given that "sensitization to allergens during infancy increases lifetime risk of developing allergies."

10. J. P. Allen, M. M. Schad, B. Oudekerk, and J. Chango, "What Ever Happened to the 'Cool' Kids? Long-Term Sequelae of Early Adolescent Pseudomature Behavior," *Child Development* 85, no. 5 (September/October 2014): 1866–1880.

11. "New Study Sheds Light on What Happens to 'Cool' Kids," Eureka Alert!, Public Release, June 12, 2014, http://www.eurekalert.org/pub_releases/2014-06/sfri-nss060514.php.

12. We say "nearly" any home because Zillow doesn't appear to track every home in the U.S., based on data we compared from the *American Housing Survey* from the U.S. Census Bureau. (The United States Census Bureau, *American Housing*

Survey (AHS), last revised May 14, 2015.) That said, the differences we found could be due to time (the data was collected approximately two years apart), or due to definitions in terms of what constitutes a "housing unit" (for the bureau) versus a "home" (for Zillow). The data we looked at includes: Table C-01-AH, *American Housing Survey,* accessed August 6, 2015, http://www.census.gov/ programs-surveys/ahs/data/2013/national-summary-report-and-tables---ahs -2013.html. This number is itself based on a sample of 70 million housing units. We also looked at "Zestimate," Zillow website, accessed August 6, 2015, Zesti-mate_Accuracy_2015_03_31, http://www.zillow.com/zestimate/#what.

13. Zillow offers quite a bit of information about its Zestimates—including a down-loadable Microsoft Excel spreadsheet that shows their accuracy (we found the link here: http://www.zillow.com/zestimate/) and a website dedicated to data ("Zillow Real Estate Research," Zillow website, accessed August 6, 2015, http:// www.zillow.com/research/data/).

14. Kenneth R. Harney, "Inaccurate Zillow 'Zestimates' a Source of Conflict Over Home Prices," *Los Angeles Times* website, February 8, 2015, http://www.latimes .com/business/realestate/la-fi-harney-20150208-story.html.

15. Keep in mind that real estate agents may have less to lose than you do when it comes to reducing the price of your house. For example, if your house sells for $300,000, your agent might get $5,250 (a 7 percent listing fee = 3.5 percent for the buyer's agent, and 3.5 percent for the seller's agent; of that 3.5 percent, half may go to the agent, and half to the agency, so each agent ends up with 1.75 per-cent). If you lower the price of your house and it sells for $250,000, your agent only loses $875 (1.75 percent of $50,000) but you've lost a lot more.

16. David Howell, "How Accurate Is Zillow's Zestimate? Not Very, Says One Washington-Area Agent," *Washington Post* website, June 10, 2014, http:// www.washingtonpost.com/blogs/where-we-live/wp/2014/06/10/how-accurate -is-zillows-zestimate-not-very-says-one-washington-area-agent/.

17. The study found that initial Zestimates "were within 5 percent of the ultimate sale price 46 percent of the time," while real estate agents' initial list prices were within 5 percent "76 percent of the time." Stan Humphries, "How Accurate Is the Zestimate? Zillow Says the Tool Is Helpful When Used the Right Way," *Washington Post* website, June 10, 2014, http://www.washingtonpost.com/ blogs/where-we-live/wp/2014/06/10/how-accurate-is-the-zestimate-zillow -says-the-tool-is-helpful-when-used-the-right-way/.

18. Note that we looked at data from a specific day, and that the values may have changed between then and whenever you're reading this.

19. Zillow says stars are "tied to" the median error rate. In the data we reviewed, a median error rate of 5.3 percent to 7.4 percent got four stars, 7.6 percent to 8.9 percent got three stars, 9.1 percent to 11.8 percent got two stars; and areas with one star didn't have a median error rate given.

20. Including a four-star rating and the lowest median error rate for top metro areas, which was 5.0 percent when we reviewed it on September 1, 2015 (last updated August 26, 2015). "Zestimate," Zillow website.

21. "Zestimate," Zillow website. Although we should note that Zillow does offer a Zestimate forecast for some properties (http://www.zillow.com/blog/zestimate-forecast-151664/), and it has a Zillow Home Value Index (http://www.zillow.com/home-values/) that offers predictions about the housing market.

INDEX

ACKNOWLEDGMENTS

This book is only possible because of the many, many people who believed in us and supported us along the way.

A number of colleagues and friends have offered invaluable insight and specific comments on the manuscript along the way, including Neal Berger, Steve Bronars, Jeffrey Brown, Courtney Coile, Derek Daniels, Ron Friedman, Kara Gorski, Bob Hoffman, Emily Oster, J. J. Prescott, Kevin Smokler, Richard Strausz, Tyler Vigen, and Justin Wolfers. A special shout-out to all of the various members of the Edgeworth lunch group, who talked about data just about every day.

Other key contributors include Geoff Barnes, Bill Ford, Rebecca Gorin-Meyer, Katie Hall, Jordan Hegyi, Frank Horowitz, Xufeng "Bill" Hua, John Jiloty, Jun Soo Kim, Mia Kim, Marty Maddin, John McKeon, Kyle Morrissey, Peter Murphy, Peter Owczarek, Casey Reinhardt, Cheryl Rudin, Joel Rudin, Rosie Sontheimer, and Ben Whitener.

You can't learn statistics and econometrics in a vacuum, and over the years John has had the benefit of being taught by several outstanding econometrics professors, including Siu Fai Leung, Jerry Hausman, Steve Pischke, and Joshua Angrist.

We're grateful to our agent, Tris Coburn, and the entire team at Bibliomotion, including Erika, Jill F., Jill S., Alicia, Ari, Shevaun, Susan, and Sue.

But we've saved the best for last. Because it's our friends and families who have been with us throughout this entire journey, watching patiently (well, mostly) as we spent countless hours seeing this through. We hope it's been worth the wait.

Mike is especially thankful for his mom and dad for their ongoing support, his brother Daniel for being a voice of reason, his kids, Zack and Ben (see guys, you get your names in a book!), and, of course, his wife, Marla, for putting up with him every step of the way.

John thanks his dad and his in-laws, Jim and Jackie, for their constant interest and excitement about this endeavor, and his brothers, Kevin and Steve (a fellow writer), for their unwavering support. He is also fortunate to have a terrific support system of friends, including Jibreel Ameen, Patrick Byrne, Jesse David, Deborah Foster, Chuck Fields, Laila Haider, Chris Johnson, Mike Kheyfets, Parker Normann, Nathan Woods, Mike Will, George Korenko, Matt Milner, and Steve Schulman. On a regular basis each of these people has engaged in endless discussions about this book. Thanks to his children, Courtney and Matthew, for really wanting to understand data because John thinks it is important (and for already preselling copies to your friends!). And, last but certainly not least, to his wife, Christie, who never fails to support him and his crazy ideas.

ABOUT THE AUTHORS

John H. Johnson, PhD, is President and CEO of Edgeworth Economics, and a professional economist, expert witness, author, and speaker. Through his leadership, Edgeworth Economics has become one of the world's premier economic consulting firms. Dr. Johnson is known internationally for his ability to explain highly sophisticated concepts in a simple, straightforward manner and brings this skill to his consulting, writing, and speaking.

At Edgeworth, Dr. Johnson provides consulting and expert testimony for Fortune 100 clients, trade groups, and government agencies. In his litigation work, he guides companies and outside counsel on the appropriate use and interpretation of complex data sets, and has served as an expert witness in some of today's most high-stakes corporate lawsuits. On the business analytics side, Dr. Johnson helps companies translate their complex internal data sets into strategic, actionable information across a variety of business settings including human resources, finance, marketing, manufacturing, and business intelligence. Both aspects share the need to understand—and properly apply—large, complex sets of data. He applies this same skill to his writing and speaking, where he helps audiences avoid common pitfalls people make when confronted with data, so they can become more confident and discerning consumers of data and make better decisions in their professional and personal lives.

Dr. Johnson is a frequent presenter on economic topics and the use of data, and has also authored numerous papers across his areas of expertise.

Dr. Johnson received a PhD in Economics from the Massachusetts Institute of Technology and his BA in Economics with Highest Distinction from the University of Rochester. He lives with his wife and two children in McLean, Virginia.

Mike Gluck is an award-winning writer who makes complex topics easy to understand. He works closely with leading organizations nationwide to translate their business goals into impactful marketing communications.

Mike's experience includes copywriting for advertising, websites, videos, annual reports, and other marketing materials, as well as editorial writing of blogs, articles, and opinion pieces. His clients are in some of today's most challenging industries, including healthcare, higher education, manufacturing and technology-related fields. Through Mike's natural curiosity, eye for detail, and strategic mindset, he is able get to the root of what needs to be said and find the language that delivers it efficiently and effectively.

Mike graduated with honors from Johns Hopkins University. He lives in Amherst, New York with his wife and two children.

John H. Johnson, PhD
EVERYDATA Keynotes

EVERYDATA: Understanding the Misinformation in the Little Data You Consume Every Day

In his keynote, John shows audiences how to recognize the misinformation buried inside the "little data" that we consume all day, every day. By providing an engaging, easily understandable, and often humorous overview of basic statistical analysis techniques, coupled with real-world examples that show their relevance in our daily lives, John gives his audiences the tools and the confidence to be smarter and more discerning in their approach to data.

EVERYDATA in the Workplace: Making Better Decisions with the Data You Consume Every Day At Work

The reality is that most of us are not trained as data experts or statisticians—but many of us are required to make data-based decisions in our jobs on a daily basis. Sometimes these decisions are small, while other times they can be costly. Think about the faulty market analysis that results in a significant capital investment, or misinterpreted production data that causes a product to be dramatically under- or over-priced. Or, an investment advisor who loses millions of dollars because he overestimated his ability to predict the future. In this address, John works with your audience to understand what conclusions can (and cannot) be drawn from the data you routinely work with, and what questions to ask so you make better, fact-based decisions.

To invite John to speak or learn more about the
EVERYDATA keynotes, visit John at JohnHJohnsonPhD.com

Learn more about Mike Gluck and Gluckworks

Mike Gluck is an award-winning writer who specializes in making complex topics easy to understand.

Mike works with leading organizations nationwide to translate their business goals into impactful marketing communications. Beyond coauthoring *EVERYDATA*, his experience includes copywriting for advertising, websites, videos, annual reports, and other marketing materials, as well as editorial writing of blogs, articles, and opinion pieces.

His clients are in some of today's most challenging industries, including healthcare, higher education, manufacturing and technology-related fields. Through Mike's natural curiosity, eye for detail, and strategic mindset, he is able get to the root of what needs to be said and find the language that delivers it efficiently and effectively.

To see how Mike can help you best reach your audience,
visit him at Gluckworks.com